Effective Small Group Communication

Second Edition

Ernest G. Bormann
Nancy C. Bormann

Effective ∗
Small ∗
Group ∗
Communication

Second Edition

By **Ernest G. Bormann,** University of Minnesota
Nancy C. Bormann, Normandale Community College

∗

∗

∗

Burgess Publishing Company • **Minneapolis, Minnesota**

Effective Small Communication contains material
originally published in *Workbook for Work Groups.* Copyright,
1966, by Ernest G. Bormann. Published by Gordon Press, Minneapolis.

10 9 8 7 6 5 4 3 2

Preface

The second edition of *Effective Small Group Communication* contains the same basic core of information about the dynamic process of good groups, about leadership, and about planning for and participating in meetings which made the first edition a useful and popular text for courses in speech communication, psychology, education, business, and for workshops in continuing education.

The authors have supplemented the basic core by enlarging the second edition substantially in the areas of small group communication theory, considerations of the task dimension of group process, conflict management, listening, public discussions, task-oriented small groups in the organizational context, and the influence of cooperation and competition on small group communication.

The book contains an entirely new section dealing with the task dimension of group process, which presents a descriptive account of how groups process information, solve problems, and make decisions based upon the latest research findings. The new section also discusses the organizational context for group meetings, the way context influences intergroup communication, and the use of groups for negotiations, creativity, and public discussion programs.

The book has been reorganized so that both the theoretical material relating to differences among the communication styles of group meetings and the scientific description of group processes appear at the beginning of the book and provide a framework for the sections of application which follow.

The second edition of *Effective Small Group Communication* retains the concise, concrete, and jargon-free style of the first edition. Each section begins with a statement of objectives and concludes with a review of key ideas. Although the material continues to present the conclusions of the most recent research in small group communication, the authors' style is such that the beginning student can grasp and appreciate the implication of all of the discoveries. The second edition keeps the first edition's balance between descriptions of group process and practical application of theoretical material to daily problems of group work.

Contents

Introduction, 2

PART I: SMALL GROUP COMMUNICATION

The Concept of Communication Styles, 6
The Styles of Small Group Communication, 7
Small Group Communication Theory, 15
The Problem of Effective Message Style Communication, 21
Communicating Through Meetings, 23
Planning the Meeting, 26
Listening, 27
A Brief Review of Key Ideas in Part I, 33
Check Your Grasp of Small Group Communication, 37

PART II: THE DYNAMICS OF GOOD GROUPS

Definition of a Work Group, 44
The Proper Size for Good Groups, 44
Groups Must Socialize As Well As Work, 45
Groups Must Work As Well As Socialize, 47
Evaluating the Work Group, 47
Cohesiveness, the Key to Successful Work Groups, 48
Group Process, 49
Building Cohesive Groups, 58

Seven Concrete Steps to Greater Cohesiveness for Your Work
    Group, 70
Building a Positive Social Climate, 72
Conflict Management in the Small Group, 76
A Brief Review of Key Ideas in Part II, 89
Check Your Grasp of the Dynamics of Good Groups, 93

PART III: LEADERSHIP

The Role of the Leader, 100
The Way Leaders Emerge, 102
The Lessons of Leadership Emergence, 105
Seven Concrete Steps to Natural Leadership, 109
Formal Leadership, 111
Techniques for Leading the Meeting, 115
A Brief Review of Key Ideas in Part III, 120
Check Your Grasp of Leadership, 123

PART IV: THE TASK DIMENSION OF GROUPS

An Unrealistic Picture of Group Work, 130
A Realistic Picture of Group Work, 131
Groups in an Organizational Context, 136
Groups in Other Contexts, 148
A Brief Review of Key Ideas in Part IV, 151
Check Your Grasp of the Task Dimension of Groups, 155

Checklist 1—Before the Meeting, 157
Checklist 2—After the Meeting, 158
Checklist 3—Your Own Leadership, 159

Sources, 161

Index, 163

I

Introduction

The college student in today's highly organized urban society often finds himself communicating in small groups for several hours each day. We live in a time when group techniques are widely used to teach many different subjects. Instructors often put students in groups to work on assignments. More and more, teachers are encouraged to break classes into smaller groups for instruction by modular scheduling in high schools and by experimental and flexible programming in junior, community, and liberal arts colleges. Students often informally get up small groups to study for examinations or to prepare for classes.

Much of our recreational and social life is related to groups. Think through your last week. How many times did you take part in casual social conversations with other people? How often did you go with a group to a party, a concert, or a movie? Groups are often used to increase understanding of social give-and-take and make people more sensitive to one another. Some groups, such as sensitivity and encounter sessions, are designed to increase individual understanding of group process and personal potential. The groups set up to increase social awareness are similar to the therapy groups that help people with problems such as alcoholism, drug addiction, juvenile delinquency, and mental illness.

The student who has a job with a business, religious, or educational organization usually works with others in a small group. In addition, the working student takes part in business meetings, committee meetings, and conferences as part of his duties.

The committee session and business conference are really the core of any sound program of communication for an organization. The small task-oriented group meeting can tell people directly about important matters in a setting where *they can ask questions and make comments.* No form of written or pictorial communication can make this claim! In addition, the meetings of small groups can build a feeling of commitment and involvement, a sense of group and organization loyalty. The person who is part of any organization identifies more readily with a small team.

No matter what we do or where we live, in a highly developed country we will find ourselves spending much of our time in work groups. Basic to successful participation in these groups is our skill in and our understanding of small group communication. The focus of this book is upon productive participation in groups that are set up to do a job.

Part I   ✳ ✳ ✳ ✳

Objectives

After you have studied Part I you should be better able to:

* *examine a group meeting and decide in what communication style the group members are participating.*

* *consider a group that you will be part of and estimate ahead of time what would be the most appropriate style for it.*

* *analyze a group meeting in terms of the ideal model of message communication for high fidelity transmission of information and evaluate its strengths and weaknesses.*

* *analyze a group's process in terms of the scientific emergent model of development.*

* *plan task-oriented group meetings.*

* *listen more carefully in both the message communication and the relationship communication styles.*

* *use checklist 1, p. 157, to make a good plan for a meeting.*

Small Group Communication

WE ARE OFTEN MISTAKEN ABOUT HOW GROUPS, in fact, work. Most people are unaware of the basic communication theory which includes the scientific descriptions of the dynamics that invariably affect group effort. In addition, we are often mistaken about the expectations of others as to the nature of a specific group meeting. We do not know what style of communication is appropriate to a given communication context. Small group communication theory consists of both scientific descriptions and stylistic rules and norms. A professional approach to small group communication requires more than formulas, rules of thumb derived from trial and error, and some conventional wisdom about how groups work. To be able to anticipate and to understand working with a group, we need to know some basic small group communication theory.

Part I presents the basic communication theory related to small groups in the most important contexts in our culture. The following section considers such basic questions as: What are the major styles of small group communication and how do they differ? How can I tell a good group when I participate in one? What is the best scientific account of the way group roles, norms, culture, and decisions emerge? How can one best design and administer group meetings? How can one improve listening skills for small group communication?

The Concept of Communication Styles

Communication style defined. A communication style is a common and generally accepted way of communicating which is understood and shared by a community of people. Style, in this sense of the term, refers to a set of expectations which all those who have learned to *appreciate* the style understand. A common meaning for the term *style* is a given individual's unusual, distinctive, and characteristic way of communicating, but what we have in mind here is not this but a generally understood manner of communicating which is shared by a number of people and which governs their behavior.

The nature of a communication style. Communication styles evolve because groups of people begin to speak in distinctive ways which are unlike the communication styles currently in vogue. People need to discuss their communication experiences in order to understand and appreciate them, and critical comments (even such "gut level" responses as "I think that was a waste of time" or "Wasn't that a great meeting!") are necessary and common at the early stage of development of a communication style. As soon as people attach labels of "good" or "bad" to the kind of communication being discussed, some standards have begun to be shared. After the pioneer groups have developed norms of communication, their members begin to criticize their communication according to the new standards or norms in a more analytical and detailed manner.

Once people understand the new style well enough to criticize communication according to its standards, they are well on their way to developing a *communication theory*. The communication theory required for the study and criticism of a style consists of (1) a description of the ideal communication event—a model, (2) descriptions of group processes that always take place no matter what the style, and (3) statements giving advice on how to approximate or achieve the ideal communication transactions.

Because the core of the theory related to a communication style is a model of the ideal communication event, you must always be taught how to communicate effectively in that style. Although we all learn how to communicate at a very early age and it thus seems as natural as walking, we cannot *just be natural* and take effective part in group meetings. Take something that is more uncommon than speaking and listening, such as learning how to appreciate, breed, and show pedigreed dogs. You cannot learn to appreciate show dogs until you have learned the basic model or ideal characteristics of a good show dog within a given breed. You must always study and learn the ins and outs of any stylized human activity in the same way. In a much more important, but similar, fashion (because communication is more important than breeding dogs), you must always learn how to participate, criticize, and theorize in a communication style by observing communication, taking part in it, reading theoretical books about it, and getting coaching from someone who thoroughly understands and appreciates the style.

The Styles of Small Group Communication

Communication styles have varied through time (a good group meeting in 1776 might well have been different from a good group meeting in 1976), from place to place (a good group meeting in West Africa might well be different from a good group meeting in northern Europe), from culture to culture (a good group meeting in a black urban ghetto in the 1960s might well differ from a good group meeting on an Indian reservation in the 1960s). But even within the mainstream of a geographical region and a general culture such as North America in the 1970s, different communication styles will thrive side-by-side. Our analysis here will deal with three major styles of small group communication common to North America in the latter part of the twentieth century. The three styles are (1) the message communication style, (2) the relationship communication style, and (3) the conversion communication style. Other styles are important, but these three are most widespread and significant, particularly in small group communication.

The message communication style. The most important communication style for people working in task-oriented small groups (that is, meetings in which the participants work together on some common task) began in the years before World War II. Engineers had for some time been working on communication problems related to the sending and receiving of messages by telephone, radio, and television, when scientists at such places as Harvard, Pennsylvania State University, the Bell Telephone Laboratories, and the Massachusetts Institute of Technology began to work on "thinking machines." The engineers tended to blueprint their plans for radios, television sets, and computers. One of the first important descriptions of a model communication event took the form of an electronic blueprint and was published by Shannon and Weaver in a book called *The Mathematical Theory of Communication* (Urbana, Illinois: University of Illinois Press, 1949). Shramm, who was interested in applying scientific research methods to mass communication, adapted the Shannon and Weaver description (W. L. Shramm, ed., *The Proccesses and Effects of Communication,* Urbana, Illinois: University of Illinois Press, 1954), and Berlo made further modifications in ·the Shramm model which resulted in a complete description that was abstract enough to cover much human as well as machine communication (*The Process of Communication,* New York: Holt, Rinehart and Winston, 1960).

The basic model of communication comes from the way humans talk to machines. Assume that we want to talk to a computer. We first clarify our thinking as to what we want to have the machine do and what information we want to communicate to it. We next make a plan of how best to get the machine to do what we want it to do and then draft a message which puts the plan into statements in machine language. We punch the statements onto cards and feed them into a computer. The machine reads the cards and either understands the message completely or does not understand it at all. Computers are very simple-minded in that they will not understand a sentence that is not written in exactly the right form, and a programmer must explain every little detail in step-by-step fashion when giving the machine directions.

As you might expect, engineers trying to communicate with the newly invented computers often failed to get their messages across. Since the persons talking to the machines could make any number of mistakes, such as failing to punctuate properly, using words the computer did not know, or failing to provide every step in a set of directions, they often had a difficult time finding the trouble. Some of the pioneers made a breakthrough when they figured out ways to have the computer give clues as to the kind of problem it was having with the message.

Once the people working with thinking machines discovered how to make the computers indicate the trouble with the message, they were able to make corrections quickly and speed up the communication process. The engineers needed a term for the process of having the computer help the programmer straighten out the message to assure complete understanding, and they picked one that was common to the study of electronics, *feedback.*

Feedback became a core principle for a whole new field of study devoted to communication and information processing. As the field expanded it came to include the way humans set goals and control behavior and the way machines can come to serve the same functions. The people involved in the new field came to call it *cybernetics.* In addition to computers, specialists in cybernetics work with information-processing systems, with automatic machines, with the automation of factories, and so forth.

The principle of feedback is at work in such simple control devices as the thermostat which controls the temperature in a room. A human being sets the temperature at a certain desired point (the goal) and after that can turn the continuous control of the heat over to the machine. The thermostat has a sensing device which measures the actual temperature and then compares it to the goal temperature. When the actual temperature is lower than the goal, for instance, the thermostat sends out an electrical message to the furnace which turns it on and adds more heat until the room temperature reaches the goal level, at which point the thermostat sends another message and turns off the heat.

One important feature of the feedback loop is that only one person, machine, or control device has the goal. The computer does not have a goal of its own and thus does not fight with the programmer over what they ought to do together as they communicate. In the ideal message communication situation, feedback is information that enables the person with the goal to achieve the intent by continuously providing the speaker with a reading on how much the listener understands.

The communication theory that is part of the message communication style has a set of standards that one can use to evaluate a given instance of communication and decide whether it is good or bad. The basic standard is the question: Was the information transmitted clearly? The technical term for clear and complete sending of information is fidelity. High fidelity tape or record players (hi-fi sets) give the listener a reproduction of more of the original sound than do record players of low fidelity. The good message communication events are those in which much of the meaning is received without distortion or loss of information.

The relationship communication style. The 1960s in America saw a reaction against science, not on the part of everybody, but by a large number of people. For the people beginning the new communication practices which were to provide an alternative style, the scientific bias of message communication was one of its shortcomings. They found the idea of control, particularly the control of one human being by another, distasteful. They saw such control as a core part of the communication model in which a message source tried to transmit information to a message receiver and often tried to control the response. The development of humanistic psychology, the human potential movement, and interpersonal communication all came together to form a new style of communication. While the message communication style emphasized communication as a means to some other end, the new relationship communication style emphasized communication as a positive value in and of itself.

A person in the message communication style talks to transmit information, to enable groups of people to cooperate to do large-scale tasks, to allow corporations and organizations to work more efficiently. The person in the relationship communication style talks and listens, for personal growth and satisfaction or to make contact with another human being.

The relationship communication style has a theory which also includes as an important part of its content a description of good communication. The theory does not use the device of a schematic model to describe the ideal, however. Theorists in the new style were often rebelling against science, and they did not use mathematical formulas, schemata, or blueprints as ways to describe good communication.

Interestingly enough, the new communication style continued to use the term *feedback* to describe an important feature of the new communication, but as the theorists developed the concept, it turned out to mean something quite different from what it means in the message style. In the relationship style *feedback* refers to the verbal and nonverbal responses that express reaction to another person, or feelings about the other person, or a response to another's communication. The statement "I didn't get any feedback" in the relationship style, means that no one responded to me or to what I said.

A key principle of the relationship style is: "You cannot not communicate." The principle means that all responses to a person in a communication event can be interpreted (and often are) in terms of relationships, feelings, and attitudes. For the message communication style with its emphasis on high fidelity transmission of information, the notion that you cannot not communicate is simply wrong; you only need to look around you to see many situations in which the model of good communication as high fidelity transmission of information is not achieved. If we define information in terms of the meanings which the message source intends to get across, then good message communication is not achieved many times. People often misunderstand, get partial or faulty information, or sometimes no information at all from messages.

For participants in the relationship style, however, the principle that "You cannot not communicate" points up their central rejection of purposive, intentional communication aimed at control of the listener. The theory of the relationship style is concerned, therefore, with both intentional and unintentional behavior which others interpret as meaningful. If a person has been sitting quietly in a meeting because she is thinking about a disturbing fight she has just had with a good friend, others in the meeting might observe her silent behavior and decide that she is uninterested in them or dislikes them. The quiet member might protest, "I didn't mean that at all!" The participants in the relationship style, however, would assert, "Whether you meant it that way or not, that is the way you came across to us."

As a result of broadening the scope of communication to include people reading unintended meanings into behaviors, the theorists of relationship communication are much concerned with a broad range of *nonverbal* communication. Where do people sit or stand in relationship to one another? What sorts of clothes do they wear? What are their hairstyles? How do they walk? How do they gesture? Are they tense? Are they relaxed? How close are they to one another when they speak? Do they touch? What does touching communicate and how? What do smells communicate?

The communication theory that goes with the relationship style describes the ideal communication event in a much different way than does the message communication theory. The relationship theory presents the process of good communication as a dialogic transaction in which the participants cease to play games with one another and are real and honest in their communication. They take risks and reveal their authentic selves. They no longer wear masks and play roles which make them less than fully human and which shield them from contact with others. They are open and welcome human contact. They disclose their feelings to one another.

The relationship theory emphasizes the basic principle of self-disclosure as a key to a warm and trusting social climate. Very active listening tends to support self-disclosing comments. People often have trouble talking about themselves honestly, but, once risked, the self-disclosing communication tends to open up others and they, in turn, disclose. The emotional tone of the communication is warmed by openness and honesty. In the warm and trusting climate of good relationship communication, people can discover their authentic selves, can grow in awareness, can raise their consciousness to higher levels. They can express their feelings, cry and laugh without worry of acceptance or rejection.

A strong and good self-image is an important ingredient in the ideal relationship communication event. One way to build a good self-image is for a person to self-disclose to others who listen empathetically and give back honest evaluation (called *feedback*), which provides the basis for the individual to evaluate himself or herself and thus have a basis for learning, change, and growth. In the ideal situation the end result is a stronger self-image, a greater sensitivity to others as people, and deep, satisfying relationships among the participants.

The heightened awareness of the relationship communication style also includes an emphasis on the senses. The ideal is to be alive and to communicate with the entire body and all the senses. The theory stresses that nonverbal communication is more authentic than verbal and more honestly expresses one's feelings. The verbal codes tend to deal in content while the nonverbal cues reveal feelings and relationships.

The student of relationship communication often discovers the nature of good communication by participating in discussions which deal with the general model of good relationship communication and by participating in special exercises, games, or group sessions and experiencing the joys of communicating in the style. Training sessions often stress feeling, touching, smelling, and other nonverbal communication exercises.

The conversion communication style. Some early students of small groups, such as Kurt Lewin, tried to make practical applications of laboratory findings. One of the early efforts was the use of small group discussions as ways to encourage behavior supporting the war effort during World War II. One pioneering study in the use of groups as persuasive devices was an investigation of ways to influence American housewives to use more visceral meat (organs such as the liver and kidney) in their cooking during the wartime meat shortages. Lewin's work was also important in the development of *group dynamics,* an attempt to apply research findings to practical problems of working with groups. Group dynamics and sensitivity training as developed by the National Training Laboratories at Bethel, Maine, were forerunners of the relationship style.

Following the lead of Lewin and his associates, a number of investigations examined the persuasive advantages of having people discuss a course of action and agree to a change in behavior in a group session as compared to such techniques as listening to a speech or reading a written persuasive message. Such studies generally found that group pressures resulted in significantly greater behavioral changes than other forms of persuasion.

In the 1960s the ferment of political and social reform and revolution in segments of the American public was accompanied by development of a number of new and distinctive communication styles. The relationship style was one such product of the period. Another small group communication style which came to prominence at about the same time was one which used small group processes for persuasive purposes.

Intensive small group sessions in many respects similar in emotional tone to groups in the relationship style, but quite different in purpose and theory, evolved to sustain political revolutionaries such as the Weatherman faction of the Students for a Democratic Society, social revolutionaries such as Gay Liberation, and reform efforts such as Women's Liberation. The women's movement has made the greatest use of the style and its participants have come to refer to the meetings as "consciousness raising sessions."

The ideal communication event in the conversion communication style is one in which the participants achieve emotional, dedicated commitment to the position advocated by the sponsoring movement. The meetings are organized around three phases of conversion. The first phase is a discussion of feelings and experiences, the second an analysis that is meaningful because the group members develop it themselves, and the third an analysis that leads to strategies for action.

The ideal of the conversion style resembles, in secular form, the persuasive steps of the traditional religious revival in American history. The evangelist first convicts the listener of sin by breaking up the old foundations and forcing the individual to make a ruthless analysis of self. The listener undergoes a period of soul-searching and evaluates her or his life by the standards of the new consciousness and finds it wanting. The speaker urges a willing faith and acceptance of the new world view, which results in the listener suddenly feeling peace and security, joy and happiness; the act of faith and willing acceptance bring the "born again" convert to a new life-style.

The conversion style of small group communication consists of groups which vary from about five to fifteen members who meet regularly, often weekly, for a period of months in *consciousness raising* sessions. The organizers and facilitators try to develop norms which encourage the participants to give personal testimony which reveals the repressive nature of society. The sharing of experiences should arouse strong feelings of anguish and rage. The members discover they are not misfits or sick and that they are facing similar problems because of a sick society. The next phase brings the members to an emotional commitment (a raised consciousness) and turns the group's attention to an analysis of the broader society. The final phase of consciousness raising should see members taking action to change society and adopt new life-styles.

Other communication styles. Obviously there are more than three general communication styles operating within the United States. There are a number of styles related to given subcultures, ethnic and racial groups, social and political positions. The three we have discussed, however, are the most important of the mainstream North American styles related to small group communication. The message communication and relationship styles both have well-developed communication theories and are, therefore, the predominant styles taught in colleges and universities. The conversion small group style also has a coherent theory and is widely taught in continuing education, church-related educational programs, and informal workshops and seminars sponsored by various social and political movements.

Some theorists have attempted to integrate elements from

relationship and message communication theories into an eclectic, all-inclusive, theory of communication. Each style, however, is distinctive and in some respects incompatible with the other. What we suggest is that the student of small group communication should come to a clear understanding of the distinctiveness of each style and learn to appreciate one or more of the styles and be able to do so in *the appropriate context.*

In the remainder of the book we emphasize the message communication style since it contains the basic theory relevant to working in task-oriented groups and trying to do a common job. We are primarily concerned with effective small group communication in organizational work groups, committee meetings, conferences, briefing sessions, decision-making meetings, and problem-solving discussions. However, task-oriented small groups can come into relationship conflicts and have other relationship problems which begin to hamper productive work norms. When task groups lose effectiveness because of interpersonal difficulties, they may well profit from a shift to the relationship style for a period of time to work things out. We, therefore, do discuss important concepts from the relationship style, such as defensive communication, the building of a positive social climate, and the handling of disagreements and conflicts.

Small Group Communication Theory

The ideal model of message communication. Remember that message communication is that everyday, businesslike, purposive communication in which all of us are engaged a lot of the time. We shall follow the typical pattern of presenting the model of message communication in schematic form as developed from Shannon and Weaver and modified by Shramm and Berlo. Figure 1 depicts a typical blueprint of a complete communication event. We will use the letters S-M-C-R as a key to the parts of the ideal model of message communication.

S stands for the *source* of the communication. If the college president dictates a memorandum to department chairpersons, he is the source for the communication event. The *M* represents the *message,* the actual words placed on the paper by the president's secretary. The *C* in the formula indicates the *channel* or channels through which the message moves. Most basically, each person

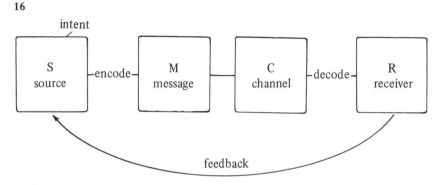

Figure 1 Ideal Model of Message Communication

receives messages through his senses—sight, smell, taste, hearing, and touch. Thus you are most likely to hear or read a message. Another set of channels consists of such paths as telephone lines, television waves, or interoffice mail. The message moves from the source through channels until it reaches the *receiver,* the *R* in S-M-C-R. Thus the president (source) sends a memorandum (message) through intercampus mail (channel) which is read (channel) by department chairperson Smith (receiver). The memorandum directs Smith to appear at 3 P.M., Thursday afternoon in conference room A for a meeting. She is told to bring the latest figures on her proposal for new instructional equipment.

The source of the communication usually makes a prediction when he sends out a message. In this case, the president predicts that Professor Smith will appear with the appropriate information at the appropriate time. If Smith fails to appear, the president is disturbed. He calls his secretary and tells her to check on Smith. She is very apologetic; it seems that Smith called in the morning to say she was sick and as the president was busy, she took the message and then forgot to tell him. The point here is that communication events are always parts of chains of communication. No sooner does a receiver get a message than she becomes the source of another message sent back through channels to the first source. Thus, a give-and-take, an interchange of messages back and forth between the people communicating with one another, characterizes the process.

Arousing meanings. Meanings are personal. Meanings, like motives, are in people. *Meanings are not in messages.* No other person has quite the same set of meanings that you have. When another person hears the word *mother,* he experiences a different meaning than you do. The problem is to get a community of meaning shared by all members of the work group. How is this done? A person, say, has a meaning he wants the group to share. He cannot put the meaning into words, speak them out of his mouth, have them carry the meaning through the air and into the ear of the listener, and then release precisely that meaning inside the head of the listener. All he can do is send out verbal and nonverbal messages that express his meaning and trust that the receiver will associate similar meanings with the messages. But the odds are very great that the first time he tries to explain himself to the group and get a community of shared meaning, he will fail.

Feedback. Here is the crux of the problem. Unless he receives a response indicating the extent of his failure, the source of a message *will assume that he has succeeded.* There's an old Spanish saying that he who keeps silent, consents. In the communication process, feedback refers to the questions, comments, facial expressions, and so forth that indicate how much the receiver understands from the message.

In terms of a work group, a member tells another something. She then watches and listens as the other member provides messages to give the speaker a reading on what the member got out of the message (what meanings it aroused in the receiver). The speaker then compares the desired level of communication with the actual and sends out additional messages designed to bring the communications on target.

For an example, take the case of two sculptors who can talk with one another by telephone but cannot see each other. One is looking at a clay statue. The other is working on a block of granite. The first describes the clay statue to the second. Together they go to work, talking back and forth, trying to get the second sculptor to approximate the clay figure in stone. It is hard work. The sculptor with the hammer and chisel must ask many questions and listen carefully. It will take considerable time, and in the end the stone statue will be only an approximation of the original clay figure.

The speaker and listener in a group are faced with a similar problem; the "statues" are meanings within each person. The source knows her meaning and tries to shape a similar one from the material available (the meanings) within the receiver. In this way, working together, the two come to a meeting of the minds. If the listener does not provide feedback to give a reading on how well the speaker is doing, the communication will fail.

The small group as a message processing system. The work group can be viewed as a message processing system. Much of the work consists of gathering, interpreting, and evaluating messages. The group then produces messages which it sends back through channels to other groups and organizations. You can place the entire group into the S-M-C-R formula as a source and receiver of messages. You can also think of each person in the group as the source and receiver of internal messages that result, more or less, in a meeting of the minds within the group. Our concern here will be with the internal face-to-face communication.

The scientific model of group process. An ideal model of communication is an extremely important part of the theory and accounts for the somewhat arbitrary and distinctive features of the various communication styles. But small group communication theory also contains descriptions of the natural, unvarying dynamics of group process which apply to all groups regardless of the style in which the participants are communicating. A descriptive model differs from an ideal model in that it describes the way groups actually work. The ideal model provides a guide for groups to follow. To return to our analogy of breeding pedigreed dogs, the descriptive model would indicate the laws of heredity, and the dog breeder would have to know them in order to change the breed systematically to approximate the ideal model he is hoping to breed.

In this section we present the descriptive model of the way groups evolve such universal features as specialization, status, and role structures, and by which they make decisions and solve problems. In Part II we will explain in detail how the emergent model explains group cohesiveness and norm development. In Part III we will use the model to explain the emergence of roles and of leadership. In Part IV we will apply the model to the way groups process information and make decisions. Here we develop the basic model in general terms.

Investigators discovered the emergent model by studying leaderless group discussions from the time they began until they had developed into structured social systems. We call such groups *zero-history groups* because the members start fresh, with no prior history or experience in working together. The groups were leaderless in the sense that the investigators did not assign any role functions such as leader, recorder, chairperson, facilitator, or moderator prior to the meetings.

Studies of these groups revealed that the communication became specialized, that some members talked more than others, and that the nonverbal communication, the message content, and the direction and flow of messages created and then reflected status differences among the members.

When the zero-history leaderless group begins to work on its task, the members have a complicated problem because not only do they have to process information and make decisions but they must also structure their group. The situation is analogous to one in which a group of people is presented with the necessary tools and supplies to build a house. They have no blueprints, however, and they have no notion as to who can do what. They are not allowed to discuss and plan how they will build the house but must begin immediately to go to work. Someone takes the initiative and makes a suggestion as to how to begin. A few may follow that person's lead and start to drive stakes to lay out a foundation. Another person may suggest a different starting place, such as first making out some plans on paper, and some may try his approach.

Both factions will take turns digging, planning, arguing, pouring concrete, sawing lumber, and so on. During the process they may discover a member with a flair for design, and that person will come to take over more and more of the major planning; they find another who is good at blueprinting, another who is good at organizing the work, several who are good at sawing and hammering, some who are good at finishing, painting, and others who do less difficult but nonetheless necessary jobs such as carrying lumber, digging foundations, mixing paint, and so forth.

When the house is completed, the group members have not only built a house, they have also come to know one another and to expect particular, specialized contributions from certain members. As a group, they have done two things almost simultaneously; they have completed their assigned task and they have completed the important job of finding leadership and a workable role structure for the group. Should they build another house, they could work more quickly and efficiently because of the structuring that took place in their first experience.

The general dynamic by which an unorganized collection of

individuals comes to be a structured and relatively stable social system is a *process of emergence.* Instead of groups deciding at first who their leader will be, they decide which members will not be leader, gradually eliminating people until a leader emerges. Instead of selecting a course of action or making a decision, the group eliminates the obviously unsuitable decisions until, gradually, the preferred decision emerges. The process is much like the one in which a photographic print emerges when it is placed in a developing solution. At first faintly, and then more clearly, one can see the outlines of the final photograph as the process continues. In much the same way, gradually, at first faintly and then more clearly, one can see the emergence of group structure and group decisions as the leaderless zero-history group develops.

The emergent model works in the following way. As the members respond to the requirements of their situation and try to go to work according to their perceptions and expectations, they respond to one another with verbal and nonverbal communication which is (1) reinforcing and supporting, or (2) ambiguous or unclear, or (3) punishing. Gradually the communications which are either supporting or punishing increase and the ambiguous responses decline. The rewards and punishments in the verbal and nonverbal messages now form a system of reinforcements which tend to encourage certain individuals to specialize and discourage others from taking on certain role functions. The system of reinforcing and rejecting messages also serves to support some decisions and negate or turn down others. The basic dynamic, however, is the same whether the group is testing role specialization or making task decisions.

The descriptive emergent model of group process is a feature of all groups regardless of their communication style. Thus message communication style groups trying to process information with high fidelity and achieve other common goals by means of the group meeting will exhibit the emergent process as will relationship style groups such as encounter and sensitivity sessions in which members build relationships and become sensitive to social processes. The emergent model also characterizes the consciousness raising session. The requirements of the various styles and the ideal model of what good group meetings ought to be like place important pressures on the members in terms of different kinds of role functions that need to be developed. But within the overall stylistic constraints, the natural dynamic of group processing functions to create specialization and status and to govern group decisions.

The Problem of Effective Message Style Communication

Some do not want to communicate. Not all message sources have successful communication as their basic purpose.

(1) *Some use language to confuse.* They try to beg the question. If they have something to hide, they would rather have the others confused than informed.

(2) *Some use language to show off.* They try to gain status as experts by using technical jargon. They prefer not to be questioned.

(3) *Some use language from habit.* They are like robots. Turn them on and certain habitual records begin to play. How are you? Isn't it exciting? The weather has been very nice. How wonderful.

Some fail to provide feedback. Even with the best intentions in the world, communication is difficult.

Recently the Small Group Communication Seminar at the University of Minnesota made intensive case studies of the failure to communicate information. The main problem in this failure turned out to be that *the person who did not know, did not ask.* Very seldom during the first discussions did anyone say, "I'm sorry, but I don't know about that. Could you tell me more?" Studies conducted by Professor Bales at Harvard University, which counted every question and every statement in a large number of meetings, indicate that group communication is characterized by *answers looking for questions.* The discussions of the Harvard students were composed of about one-third questions and two-thirds answers.

Why don't people provide feedback by asking questions when they don't understand? We already know, of course, that during the struggle for roles, people do not want to appear ignorant and lose face (status) in the group. Often members pretended to know more than they actually did rather than ask for information. Then, too, in some of the meetings, very few questions were raised, so it just did not seem to be the thing to do.

Some fail to listen. During the period of the "shakedown cruise" people often cannot ask a question because they have not listened to the previous comment. During the period of role testing, people are eager to demonstrate their wares. They wait for a cue from the discussion that makes them "think of something to say." They then plan how they will say it and watch impatiently for an opening. When they get the stage, they say as much as they can, as effectively as they can. When they must give up the spotlight, they try to think up another good comment. When one occurs to them, they wait for another opportunity to speak. Since people seldom listen well during the "shakedown cruise," they often say things unrelated to the topic mentioned by the previous speaker. They say what is on their minds, even if the comment is no longer pertinent, and they say as much as they can think of, even though they may introduce several ideas in one comment.

If an individual has not done well in a session, she may be disturbed enough to go over the proceedings afterwards in her mind and "replay" the meeting. During the second thinking, she will provide the good comments she could have made in order to "star."

Some show of knowledge. Showing off knowledge and demonstrating expertness are somewhat different from communicating information or explaining technical matters. The person who is primarily interested in making a good impression may talk rapidly and introduce technical words. By this tactic he hopes to impress others with his knowledge without opening himself to embarrassing questions. Most professions have developed a tradition of protecting the expertness of their members from the layman by means of a complicated vocabulary. Technical terms can serve a useful function in naming clearly defined concepts. The expert may change his purpose from defending his status to explaining technical matters. When he does so, he may still use a technical vocabulary; the change in attitude, however, should result in a change in presentation. (An expert may have developed such strong habits of defending his status that even when he wants to communicate, he no longer has the requisite skills.) Generally, a person who wants to inform will introduce the technical concepts more slowly, will define them carefully, and will encourage questions and feedback.

Communicating Through Meetings

The uses of meetings. Meetings are essential to effective communication within the modern organization. The meeting provides a chance to inform members directly about important matters. The meeting is an excellent tool to build cohesiveness. It identifies the work group and gives it a chance to develop a tradition. The meeting can provide a channel for upward communication. Meetings and discussions are also techniques for solving problems and developing policy.

The abuses of meetings. Some meetings are held for no good reason. Perhaps originally the meeting may have served a function but, as time goes by, the organization changes and the meeting loses its purpose. The meeting is held out of habit. Meetings are also used as administrative dodges. One way for an administrator to handle a touchy issue is to "bury it" in committee. Finally, an administrator may use the meeting as a smoke screen for a decision. In such an instance, he has already made up his mind, but he pretends that the meeting will have an effect on the decision. After a time, the people in the meeting catch on to what is happening. They know that the meeting is simply a show, that the "old man" has already made up his mind, and that nothing said in the meeting will change things. Such meetings are time wasters.

Kinds of meetings. Work groups use several different sorts of meetings. If they come with the wrong expectation of what kind of meeting they are attending, they may find the meeting frustrating. For example, if the meeting is ceremonial and the person who came expected it to be used to make decisions, she would feel cheated.

(1) *The ritualistic meeting.* Every organization has some meetings that are rituals. In addition to aiding the cohesiveness of the organization, these meetings assure that people of authority are recognized. For example, the department heads may make an oral presentation of their yearly budget to a meeting of all vice-presidents. The meeting puts a rubber stamp on decisions already made. Yet the meeting is important to the social interaction of the organization. The Young Turk who says this meeting accomplishes nothing and is therefore a waste of time is judging it on the wrong grounds.

(2) *The briefing meeting.* The briefing session is designed to provide members with the information to carry through on plans already laid. The objective is clear and people need only to find out who is to do what, when, and where.

(3) *The instructional meeting.* A meeting may be used to teach people in order to make them more proficient in their tasks.

(4) *The consultative meeting.* A consultative meeting is one wherein the person responsible for a decision asks the members for advice. She remains responsible for the decision, but she does ask and consider their advice.

(5) *The decision-making meeting.* One of the most difficult and yet most useful meetings is that designed to make decisions and formulate courses of action. *Members who help make, and who are responsible for, decisions are usually more fully committed to them and work harder to implement the action.*

The one-time meeting. The one-time meeting is such an important communication context that it deserves special attention. The one-time discussion meeting is different from the ad hoc committee. *Ad hoc* is a Latin term meaning "for this special purpose." An ad hoc committee is set up for a given task and usually meets for several or more sessions. For very important tasks the ad hoc may meet for a period of weeks or months. The one-time meeting, on the other hand, is held by people who expect to achieve their purpose in a single meeting. The people in the one-time meeting have not worked together before and are not likely to do so again for the purposes under discussion. The one-time meeting may take place in an organizational context but quite often people use the one-time meeting for community purposes. Representatives from several different organizations or interest groups may come to a one-time meeting to discuss a common problem, share information, or plan a joint enterprise.

Since the composition of the one-time meeting is unique, the group has no history and the members cannot be guided by past experience with one another in such a discussion. The group has no team spirit, no "usual" ways of doing things, no idea about how the communication and social interactions will go.

The ad hoc committee is like the one-time meeting in that both are zero-history groups, *but the ad hoc committee has a future*. The members look forward to having more meetings, and the influence of future expectations brings the emergent model of group process strongly into play. The zero-history group with a future is under pressure to test potential leaders and other possibly influential members, to develop norms, to take nothing at face value, to check reputations, formal organization status, and assigned structures—before accepting them.

One of the important things about the one-time meeting is the greater willingness of members to accept assigned leadership. Whether the person calling the meeting is a self-appointed moderator or has been assigned to lead by some organizational unit, the members are likely to accept and appreciate direction from that individual. The group conducting a one-time meeting needs quick help in getting started. Members realize they have little time to waste and tend to accept with little argument the assigned moderator's description of the purposes of the meeting and his or her set of procedures to get on with the meeting.

Members in a one-time meeting take shortcuts to structure their group into a pecking order so they can get on with the business at hand. They are willing to risk getting a wrong impression because they are so pressed for time and because the group is so short-lived that they often do not want to invest the time and energy it takes to allow the emergent model of group dynamics to function through to completion. Unfortunately, many members of ad hoc committees begin their group life with the same simplistic expectations and are very upset when they find themselves devoting much more time and energy to the group than they ever thought they would have to. If one agrees to serve on an ad hoc committee, he or she must understand the important distinction we are stressing here. People become *involved* when they must work on ad hoc committees, whether they "plan to" or not.

Once a one-time discussion gets under way, though, participants use any information they have about one another to structure their responses. If the participants discover one member is a graduate student in speech-communication, another is a football player, a third is a law student, and so on, they use such information to guide their expectations. The participants who are not known by reputation are quickly sterotyped on the basis of first impressions and whatever scant information others have. A person who does not say much for the first ten or fifteen minutes may be stereotyped as quiet and shy or uninterested. Another, who speaks loudly, expresses strong opinions, and makes flat judgments, may be stereotyped as bossy or pushy.

Members of a one-time meeting in mainstream North American culture tend to have a set of expectations of how a meeting should be run. In Part III we describe the common expectations of how a person should lead a one-time meeting. Here we discuss the way to plan a meeting when you are in charge of getting things ready. These procedures are appropriate to the one-time meeting as well as to the other kinds of meetings discussed above.

Planning the Meeting

Be sure you need a meeting. Do not have a meeting unless it is absolutely necessary. Meetings are the heavy artillery of an organization's communications. A wise general uses his heavy artillery sparingly because it is expensive and difficult to maneuver. On the other hand, when he does need his big guns, he really has no satisfactory substitute for them. If the communication can be handled by individual conferences, telephone conversations, memorandums, or other techniques, the meeting is probably unnecessary.

Determine the purpose of the meeting. Every meeting should have a clear and specific purpose. Make sure the others know the purpose either before the meeting starts or very early in the session.

Plan the meeting to achieve the purpose. Where is the best place to hold the meeting? What format will best achieve the purpose? Should you use a slide lecture with questions and answers for a briefing session? Would short reports from several members, followed by questions and answers, be appropriate for a consultative meeting? Could a round table discussion of an agenda be used for policy-making? Also, who should take part in the meeting? Should people with special knowledge be invited? Should some high status people be invited to keep fences mended within the organization? Who might jeopardize the outcome if she felt hurt because she was not informed or consulted? Who should chair the meeting?

Plan the little details. A successful meeting requires time and effort in the planning stages. Don't neglect the planning. You may save time for your own work that way, but wasting the time of your colleagues in a useless meeting is not wise. Little things like providing pads and pencils, refreshments, properly arranged (and sufficient) seating—all these contribute to the success of the meeting. When minor details of administration are handled smoothly, the people get the feeling that the meeting is important and that it is going to do significant work.

Specify the outcomes of the meeting. This is not the same as deciding on the purposes. If plans are to be made, how will they be developed? In detail? In general outline? Decide what decisions can be made in such a meeting and in what form they should be made.

Utilize the results of the meeting. The substantive results of the meeting should be used. What can be done to follow up and apply the results of the conference? Do not let important leads drop at the end of the meeting.

Evaluate the meeting systematically. Spend some time evaluating the effectiveness of the meeting. We always make an informal evaluation of a meeting as we walk away from it. We may say to someone else, or just to ourselves, that it was a good meeting, or that we talked all around the subject, or that it was a waste of time. Some member of the group should collect impressions of the strengths and weaknesses of the meeting. These evaluations should be fed back to the participants. One of the striking discoveries in the study of groups is that they seldom spend any time talking about the *group* and about *how it functions.* Groups tend to concentrate on the job and ignore the important matters discussed in the remainder of this book. When groups do spend short periods after the meeting talking, as a group, about what happened in the meeting, about what was good and what was bad, the cohesiveness and effectiveness of the meetings are increased. Often things that are very disturbing when hidden from others evaporate when brought out into the open and discussed. Perhaps one person with some education in group process should be asked to serve as an evaluator of the meeting, and she can present a systematic statement to start the discussion.

Listening

In order to be a successful listener in a task-oriented small group you must (1) be willing to be a message receiver, (2) know the basic communication skills of listening, and (3) practice and apply sound feedback techniques.

Playing the role of message receiver. Good high fidelity communication in the S-M-C-R model is dependent upon feedback. Feedback, in turn, requires that a message receiver provide the source with help in their joint game against confusion. When you play the role of receiver, therefore, you must, for the time that you are receiving, concentrate on the other person's objective—help the source get his or her point over to you. To be a receiver you have to forget your own point and your own wishes for the time being. To judge the quality of feedback we need to know the source's purpose or intent and then we must examine how well the feedback aids the source in bringing the response of the receiver on target. This is not the same thing as saying the receiver must always agree with the source. What the receiver must always do is give adequate feedback to the source to assure the source that he, the receiver, *has understood* the message as it was sent. Emphasis on the successful transmission of messages often puts a strain on personal relationships. If potential receivers think the message source is trying to assume a "one-up" position, they may simply refuse to listen, to be receivers in the full sense.

The target of a comment may refuse to accept the source's goal and refuse to play the role of receiver in cooperatively providing feedback. The target individual may, instead, encode messages as a source; such attempts do not function as feedback. What is worse, if the first person interprets these returning messages *as* feedback, confusion results.

When two people both try to play the role of message source and each talks to achieve his or her own personal goals, the two are not communicating according to the ideal of the S-M-C-R model. Instead, each produces a separate incomplete communication event consisting of $S_1 M_1 C_1 \ldots$ and $S_2 M_2 C_2 \ldots$ going on at the same time. We have the not unfamiliar case of two people talking past each other, or of two people talking in the presence of one another, without talking *with* one another.

Often people refer to the situation where nobody wants to be a receiver and everybody wants to be a message source as *poor listening.* A member may comment after the meeting that "Nobody was listening. We were all talking at once. We all had something to say and we didn't even hear what anybody else said. Next meeting we better start listening to one another." The problem in the situation where nobody assumes the role of receiver is not lack of listening skills so much as the unwillingness of the participants, who may be very good at listening when they put their minds to it, to take on the listening, or receiver's, role.

The first step in successful listening, therefore, is to play the role of message receiver when it is appropriate to do so.

Why do people fail to be message receivers? Often people fail to listen because of poor interpersonal relationships. If you do not know the message source, you may be ill at ease, tense, unsure, and not willing to assume the role of listener until you get better acquainted. If you are suspicious, hostile, or antagonistic to the message source you will often refuse to assume the role of receiver. You might feel that to become a listener would give the other person an advantage and you do not want to help such a person. If you become defensive in a communication situation, you will often try to assume the role of message source as a strategy of defense. The S-M-C-R ideal is a process description. All elements of the model are interrelated. The verbal and nonverbal communication of the person trying to assume the role of source is important in whether or not the others become defensive and influences their willingness to listen. Gibb discovered that certain kinds of messages tend to result in defensive responses. If the message source talks in a way which is interpreted by the others as an attempt to manipulate or to be superior, then they are unlikely to assume the role of receivers. The messages which make listening difficult include those which are (1) evaluative: *"I think you've done the wrong thing about this";* (2) controlling: *"Why don't you all go to the library before the next meeting; I want you to look up . . .";* (3) strategic: *"That sounds pretty good, but John and I were talking the other night and we wondered if maybe we couldn't . . .";* (4) neutral: *"I could care less. Just do what you want";* (5) superior: *"This happens to be my major and I just did a term paper on it. Why don't you just let me fill you in";* or (6) certain: *"Under no circumstances would I accept that."*

Our normal response to any of the above messages is to be defensive and to reject the role of receiver. Why should we willingly use feedback to help someone put us in a one-down position? Our point here is that listening is the responsibility of the speaker as well as of the potential auditor. As a person trying to get information across, playing the role of source, you need to send verbal messages, combined with nonverbal messages, that create a supportive climate in which people do not feel a need to defend themselves. When they can feel secure they can assume the role of receiver much more easily and efficiently.

As message source you can encourage listening by using messages with the following characteristics: (1) description (rather than evaluation): *"You have talked to the instructor and asked for more time on our project, is that it?"*; (2) problem orientation (rather than control orientation): *"I think we need to get some solid information"*; (3) spontaneity (rather than strategy): *"Hey! This idea just came to me"*; (4) empathy (rather than neutrality): *"At first I couldn't see why you were so excited about this but I'm beginning to understand"*; (5) equality (rather than superiority): *"We have a lot of resources in this group and if we all pool our knowledge and talent we should have a good group";* and (6) open-mindedness (rather than certainty): *"I want to look into that further before we decide."*

While the message source has considerable responsiblity in creating a suitable climate so you can more easily assume the role of receiver, the responsibility is shared. You may have to force yourself to assume the role of listener even when an inept person is sending out nonverbal messages that he or she is evaluative, manipulative, and loves to be in a one-up position. Without message receivers in a task-oriented small group, there is little chance for understanding and cooperative effort.

When participating in a group meeting you should accept the role and duties of message receiver willingly at appropriate points in your interaction. Of course, after you have come to an understanding with the speaker, you should have your chance to be the message source, and then the others should assume the role of receiver. If you anticipate conflict, you should certainly allow the source to develop a complete message first, and then you should provide feedback until both of you are satisfied that you understand one another. Many potential conflicts never develop when the two participants check out one another's meanings with suitable feedback and discover their differences are in their use of language rather than in their fundamental thinking. If you decide, however, after reaching a meeting of the minds, that there is a conflict and that you are not going to cooperate to achieve the source's intent, you ought to assert yourself clearly in the role of message source for another round of communication. The other person should then willingly assume the role of receiver until your message is understood. Understanding does not assure harmony and cooperation. Group members who understand one another may still disagree, come into conflict, or grow to dislike one another, but at least they will do so on a realistic basis and not from lack of communication skills—particularly from lack of willingness to play the role of receiver.

Basic listening skill. Once you agree to play the role of message receiver, then the basic skills of good listening come into play. Our point here is that even if you want to listen and are quite willing to play the role of message receiver, you still may not do very well at it because of lack of skill. However, listening skills can be learned and improved through practice.

To be a good listener you must learn to *focus your attention on the message.* Playing the role of receiver is a time-consuming and tension-producing job. You must exert effort to keep your attention from wandering. All too often our minds drift away from what a person is saying; we focus again for a bit and then start thinking of something else. If you missed the last sentence you read, you can go back over it again. Not so with spoken communication, particularly the kind occurring in small task-oriented groups. With practice you can learn to monitor your attention, to realize when you are fading in and out of a listening situation. You will be able to tell when your attention begins to waver, and you can pull it back to the message. To learn to monitor yourself you have to keep part of your mind on how well you are listening. You can help focus on the message, even when the source is a dull speaker who seems to be taking an extremely long time to make a point, by anticipating what the next point will be. By guessing what the source will say next, you create some suspense for yourself and you can then check to see if you were right. If you guessed correctly, you have thought about the idea twice and are more likely to have a clear understanding of it. If you guessed wrong, you can try to figure out why the speaker took that particular turn, and, again, you have been attending to what is being said. You may also combat boredom or a tendency for your mind to wander by taking out ten or twenty seconds from time to time to review what the participant has just said and how it fits into the thread of the discussion. You will find that periodic summarizing helps you understand and recall important ideas later.

To be a good listener you must learn to *structure the message.* People who listen for factual details tend to have trouble remembering the main ideas and, oddly enough, even have trouble remembering the details later. They end up with a vague idea about a mass of undigested material. We remember patterns of ideas more easily than strings of facts. Practice listening for the main outline or shape of a comment. You will find your understanding increasing. You will discover that with practice you can often take a poorly organized message and refit its parts into a better pattern. You may indeed be able to recall more of what a member said during the meeting than the source himself can, if you organize the material more effectively as you listen.

Feedback skills. Once you have agreed to play the role of message receiver, then the basic listening skills discussed above come into play. But in addition, you must develop skills in providing feedback. The good listener provides the message source with continuous feedback. The source, in turn, searches constantly for feedback and keeps sending additional messages to achieve a satisfactory level of understanding. If both source and receiver play their roles willingly and with skill, the whole process becomes a classic expression of the model of ideal message communication.

A good listener develops skill in providing both nonverbal and verbal feedback. Research in nonverbal communication indicates that facial expressions are among the most important cues to response and reaction. You should smile, frown, look puzzled, allow the moment of insight to spread over your face when you think you see what the source is driving at, and so forth. Head nods and shakes are good commonly understood ways of providing agreement and disagreement. In short, when playing the role of receiver, a good listener is as active nonverbally as the individual playing the message source is verbally, and will provide feedback continuously; the listener's cues are intentional and conscious.

A receiver's skill in providing verbal feedback is also important to successful listening. The receiver can indicate the nature of the problem verbally. "I'm confused on that point." "Let's see now if I've got this straight. What I hear you saying is . . ." "Maybe I misunderstood you. I thought that you meant . . ." Questioning is also an important skill in providing feedback. "What do you mean by *cybernetics* again?" "How do you connect up those two ideas again?" The listener can also provide feedback by repeating, echoing, or rephrasing the message. "OK, now let me repeat what I think you just said." "Here's what I understand you to be saying."

When you are in a group discussion in the message communication style you should alternate the roles of source and receiver, and when you play the role of receiver you must be willing to bide your time, listen, provide feedback, and come to a meeting of the minds with the source before you launch into your own turn at playing message source. You must try to provide feedback even if it seems to put you in a one-down position temporarily or threaten your status in the group or make you seem ignorant or unintelligent. Finally, you should take the initiative when necessary and stop the communication flow and indicate to the source verbally and nonverbally that (1) there is a problem (misunderstanding) and (2) what kind of problem it is, and (3) where you stand in terms of how confused you are or what you understand and what you do not understand.

✳

A Brief Review of Key Ideas in Part I

✳   A communication style is a common and generally accepted way of communicating that is understood by a community of people.

✳   You must always *learn* to participate, criticize, and theorize in a communication style.

✳   Communication styles may vary from time to time, place to place, and culture to culture.

✳   The message communication style emphasizes high fidelity transfer of messages.

✳   Feedback is a central concept of the message communication style and refers to the questions, comments, facial expressions, and so forth, that indicate how much a receiver understands from a message.

* The relationship communication style emphasizes communication as a positive value in and of itself.

* The person in the relationship communication event talks and listens, for personal growth and satisfaction and to make contact with another human being.

* A key principle of the relationship style is "You cannot not communicate."

* The relationship style is concerned with a broad range of nonverbal features of communication including context, gestures, positioning of participants, and vocal accompaniment to words.

* The conversion communication style uses group processes for persuasive purposes.

* The basic group meetings of the conversion style are called *consciousness raising sessions.*

* The ideal communication event in the conversion style is one in which the participants come to an emotional and dedicated commitment to the position of the sponsoring group.

* The ideal model of the message communication style consists of a source, messages, channels, and a receiver: S-M-C-R.

* A descriptive model of group process differs from an ideal model like S-M-C-R in that it describes the way groups actually work.

* To achieve communication according to the ideal, groups must work with the grain of the natural development of group process revealed by the descriptive model.

* The emergent descriptive model indicates that members of groups specialize, assume roles, and create status differences.

* Both decisions and roles emerge gradually because of a system of rewards and punishments that develops as people work cooperatively together.

* The descriptive emergent model of group process is an account of the dynamic of all groups regardless of their communication style.

* The one-time meeting is held by a group which expects to achieve its purpose in a single meeting.

* One of the important things about the one-time meeting is the greater willingness of its members to accept assigned leadership.

* Participants in the one-time meeting take shortcuts to structure their group into a pecking order so they can get on with the business at hand quickly.

* Often people refer to the situation where nobody wants to be a receiver and everybody wants to be a message source as poor listening.

* The first step in successful listening is willingness to play the role of message receiver.

* People often refuse to be message receivers because of defensiveness or because they do not want to be placed in a one-down position.

* To be a good listener you must learn to focus your attention on the message by monitoring your own listening.

* To be a good listener you must have and use good feedback skills, both nonverbal and verbal.

Check Your Grasp of Small Group Communication

*(Complete all answers, then check
each answer on the pages given.)*

1. Define *communication style.*

—pages 6 and 7

2. Describe the ideal model of communication according to the message communication style.

—pages 15 and 16

3. Give an example of feedback.

—pages 17 and 18

38

4. Describe the ideal model of communication according to the relationship communication style.

—pages 11 and 12

5. Explain the principle, "You cannot not communicate."

—page 12

6. Describe the ideal model of the conversion communication style.

—pages 13 and 14

7. Describe the emergent model of group process.

—pages 18 to 20

8. List the problems of effective message style communication.

—pages 21 and 22

9. List as many of the kinds of meetings as you can recall.

—pages 23 and 24

10. Give three examples of one-time meetings.

—pages 24 and 25

11. List as many kinds of messages that cause defensiveness as you can.

—page 29

12. List three examples of nonverbal feedback.

—page 32

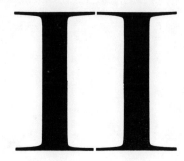

Part II　✳✳✳✳

Objectives

After you have studied Part II you should be better able to:

* *evaluate a group.*

* *estimate a group's level of cohesiveness on the basis of the way the members communicate with one another.*

* *discover the role and status structure of a group from the communication patterns.*

* *describe a group's norms in both the task and social dimensions.*

* *compute the attraction of a group for individual members by estimating the rewards and costs of the group for each.*

* *design a program of action that you can take to improve the cohesiveness of a given group.*

* *respond quickly to situations that arise in a meeting and in such a way that you help to build a positive social climate.*

* *manage group conflict more productively.*

The Dynamics of Good Groups

WE HAVE ALL WORKED WITH OTHERS before arriving at a careful, systematic study of group dynamics. Because of our previous experiences, then, we all have many ideas and beliefs about the way people work in committees which can be useful as starting places for the study of small group communication. In many ways, however, our "common sense" and vague ideas about how groups work can stand in the way of increased understanding and improved performance.

Part II contains definitions of key concepts based upon extensive study and systematic research into group process. Because we present the definitions in simple and straightforward terms, you should not conclude that we are simply restating the common sense meanings for the terms. Learn the precise definitions because they are crucial to your ability to analyze group process and to improve your participation in meetings.

Part II is devoted to the "good group" and answers such basic questions as: What is a task-oriented small group? How can I tell a good group when I see one? What makes groups tick? Why do people have personality conflicts in groups? How can I generate group loyalty? Why do groups have apathetic members?

Definition of a Work Group

A basic definition. The task-oriented small group is composed of three or more people working together to do a clearly specified job or to reach a common goal.

Two-person interview excluded. We do not deal with the dialogue, or two-person interview, because the introduction of a third person changes the nature of the working and social relationships.

Therapy groups excluded. We do not examine therapy groups, sensitivity training groups (T-groups), encounter groups, or any other groups in the relationship style. These have as their primary purpose the improvement of the mental or social health of the individual by having him work out his personal problems through the group. Our aim is to concentrate on groups with a common problem to solve or a job to do and which employ the message communication style.

Groups may be short term. Examples of short-term groups would be: a committee meeting for the PTA, a study group for the League of Women Voters, a business conference, a discussion group at a campus religious house, or a committee for a student government project.

Groups may be long term. Examples of long-term groups would be: a project team in a research and development section of a computer company, an ad hoc committee to study metropolitan problems, a student and faculty committee to study curriculum changes, standing committees of campus organizations, the basic on-the-job group where an individual earns a living, and the family.

The Proper Size for Good Groups

A good size for a group. Research on small groups indicates that five is an excellent number for a work group. Members of groups with fewer than five people complain that their groups are too small. Groups composed of an even number of people are not as efficient as groups totaling an odd number. Five or seven is a better size for a committee than four, six, or eight. Five is the dividing point. Larger groups change character and have different patterns of communication.

When groups grow larger. In groups of five or less, all participants speak to one another, even those who speak very little. In groups of seven or more, the quiet members cease to talk to one another and talk only to the top people – the leader or the high status persons. As groups get even larger, the talk centralizes more and more around a few people. Group interaction falls off. In groups of thirteen or more, a small group of from five to seven usually holds the discussion while the others simply watch and listen. In permanent work groups larger than thirteen, the tendency is to form small groups (cliques) within the larger group.

When forming a committee. If you can appoint the members to a committee or work group, be sure that you have an odd number and try to make it five or seven. If the group must be larger than seven, consider the use of subcommittees to do some of the projects.

When the work group is long term. If the permanent work group is larger than seven, watch for the formation of cliques within the larger group, and examine their development in the light of group process. These small groups can be mobilized for the good of the larger unit. The danger is that if they are disgruntled with the leadership of the larger group, they may fight its goals.

Groups Must Socialize As Well As Work

The work group is a social event. When several people share ideas or produce a product, a whole *social* dimension is added. The first question in the mind of every person in a new work group is: HOW DO I RELATE TO THESE OTHER PEOPLE AS A HUMAN BEING? Every member wants this question answered, and he wants it answered early! Moreover, even after he has been in the group for months or even years, he wants the answer repeated, however briefly, each day!

Do not ignore the social dimension of your work group. Talking about hobbies, reading habits, sports, travels, family, and friends is important to the social health of the group. If you are calling the first meeting of a new group, take a few minutes at the beginning for such talk.

(1) Have an informal "get acquainted period" scheduled during which refreshments are served. (More suitable for a committee or study group meeting in a home.)

(2) Or, begin the first meeting by having each participant talk

about himself, his interests, how he feels about an important topic under consideration.

(3) Or, adjourn the first meeting a bit early and encourage people to stick around afterwards. People often relax and feel free to say things when the meeting is over that they would not say during the first session. If it is a business meeting, you may ask the group to break for coffee in the cafeteria after the session.

If you are chairperson of a continuing group, supervisor of an office force, or president of a campus organization, take some time in each work session for similar talk.

One businessman in a communication seminar asked, "How can you justify wasting the company's time socializing on the job?" To which another executive answered, as we would have, "How can you afford not to?"

The importance of the social dimension. If a person feels that the others like, admire, and respect her, that they enjoy her company and consider her ideas important, she can let her hair down and turn her full attention to doing the job. Such an atmosphere of trust and understanding should be the goal of every participant, and *particularly* of every manager, chairperson, moderator, or leader of a work group. The group member is seldom sure about these matters, however, and as she goes about the job, talking about important problems and exchanging information, she may think that some work-related comment is a threat to her standing in the group, or to her as a person, or that it constitutes a slur on those she represents. She may feel that a comment suggesting that her committee has fallen down on the job is really a criticism of her as a person rather than an evaluation of the source of a problem. Immediately, she is on guard, preoccupied with social matters rather than with task considerations.

How important is the social dimension? Consider two groups composed of the same sorts of people and doing the same job; one can be torn with dissension, absenteeism, and low productivity, while the other, composed of members who respect each other, may work harmoniously and effectively. What is the difference? For the most part, you can say one has a healthy social dimension and the other has not.

Groups Must Work As Well As Socialize

The work group is a task event. We are only discussing those groups that have a job to do. Inevitably the members will expect to, and usually want to, concentrate on the job. If the group is meeting for a discussion or conference, they will want to get to the agenda and start talking about it. If the group is a message-processing unit, the members will want to start reading the mail, absorbing the memorandums, filing important papers, drafting letters, holding conferences, and so forth. If it is a political action group, the members will want to lay plans and get organized.

Working with others is more difficult than working alone. We usually enjoy having company while we work, but coordinating effort is difficult. Handling ideas in a group meeting is not a simple task. Working with several people to achieve a common goal complicates matters. Do not expect a group to work with the same concentration and efficiency as one good individual working alone. Groups require structure and coordination. Coordination takes efficient planning and communication. The group's ability to concentrate its talents and energy on the task, its ability to mobilize its resources, will be hampered by poor plans, misunderstandings, faulty reasoning, inadequate concepts, bad information, and, most importantly, by the way directions and orders are given and received. *A whole book could be devoted to the subject of giving and receiving orders.* Orders must be given, but when you give another person an order, the task and social areas come into conflict. If the group member thinks the direction is an indication that the leader feels superior to him or that he is using the group for his own purposes, the order may be misunderstood or not obeyed, even though it is a good one.

Evaluating the Work Group

Evaluate the social health. A good work group has high morale. The members are happy with the group. They enjoy working with the others on the job and are pleased with their place in the group. They receive a sense of belonging and a feeling of personal satisfaction from their role.

Evaluate the productivity. A good group gets things done. It reaches its goals with a minimum of wasted motion. It turns out a large quantity of high quality work, wins games, solves problems, makes good decisions.

Balance both the social health and the productivity. Some people think that productivity is all that counts. But the individual should gain a sense of satisfaction and worth from participation in the group. We do not believe that the individual exists solely for the group. The group has certain duties and responsibilities to the individual.

Cohesiveness, the Key to Successful Work Groups

Cohesiveness defined. Cohesiveness refers to the ability of the group to stick together. Another term for the same quality is *group loyalty.* A highly cohesive group is one in which the members work for the good of the group. They help one another and exhibit team spirit. They reflect the motto of Alexandre Dumas' *Three Musketeers,* "All for one and one for all."

Cohesiveness encourages productivity, morale, and communication. Groups with high group loyalty have greater productivity, higher morale, and better communication than groups with little cohesiveness.

(1) Cohesive production groups do more work because members take the *initiative* and help one another. They distribute the work load among themselves. They take up the slack in times of stress. Workers in groups with little cohesiveness tend to stand around and wait for assignments from their supervisors. They do only what they are told to do and no more. They do not care about the work of the others. While members of cohesive groups volunteer to help one another, people in groups with little cohesiveness "keep their noses clean" and "look out for number one."

(2) The morale of the members is closely tied to the cohesiveness. If the group is important to them, people pay attention to its problems. They spend time and effort in behalf of the group, and they glory in its successes.

(3) The more cohesive the group, the more efficient the communication within the group. Cohesiveness encourages feedback, disagreements, and questions. Members of highly

cohesive groups indicate when they do not understand, and disagree among themselves. They cannot stand by and watch the others do a shoddy job or make a wrong decision. Their group is at stake. They must speak up and do what they can to assure its success. Such disagreements improve the quality and quantity of the work by assuring a high level of communication. Cohesiveness encourages feedback. In the cohesive group, every member knows his place and is secure. His position is not threatened if he admits that he does not know something. Indeed, the welfare of the group requires that each member have adequate information. The group rewards feedback that helps it achieve its goals. Likewise, the important member does not feel insulted when people pin him down and ask for more information. He is more interested in the welfare of the group than in his own personal feelings. Since the group largely succeeds or fails depending upon the efficiency of its communication, the cohesive group encourages its members to work cooperatively to come to a meeting of the minds.

The symptoms of low cohesiveness. Groups with little cohesiveness have meetings which are quiet, polite, boring, and apathetic. The general attitude of the members is reflected by their tense posture, their sighs and yawns. Their attitude is, "Let's get this meeting over with. I am uncomfortable." People seldom disagree; there is little give-and-take discussion. Often a question is followed by a long pause. Even important decisions are handled quickly, with little comment.

The symptoms of high cohesiveness. Work meetings of highly cohesive groups tend to be noisy, full of joshing, personal byplay, disagreement, and even argument. They often run overtime and people may continue the discussion after the meeting is over. Few important questions are raised without a thorough airing.

Group Process

Research in small groups. We are now going to come to the heart of the matter: what makes the group tick. What follows is not going to be simple, but it is absolutely essential for an understanding of work groups. Group process is complex — not difficult, but complex.

The difference between our approach now and the helpful-hints treatment of conference leadership is that we will explain some of the results of the most recent basic research in group process. Sociologists and psychologists did not discover work groups until relatively recently. A. Paul Hare collected a list of studies of small groups from 1890 to 1958 and found that from 1890 to 1899, there was about one study published every two years. Nowadays hundreds of research studies of small groups are published every year.

Why so much interest in basic research on groups? The Second World War was a turning point. The war put a premium on productivity and morale in business, industry, and the armed services. We had to produce. Millions of dollars were spent by government and industry to study the factors that go into productivity. The dynamic factors within a small group proved extremely important to both concerns.

The test-tube group. One of the important techniques used to study group process was the test-tube group. The studies in group process, communication, and leadership at the University of Minnesota have used this approach. The test-tube groups are composed of strangers and are set up under carefully controlled conditions. The groups have no formal structure. Every member is a peer — that is, they are all equals. They do have a clear job and a specific time limit. In the test-tube groups, the normal operations of a work group are speeded up by "pressure cooker" methods. The basic patterns of group process appear quickly and without distracting variables, so they may be discovered and charted.

Role specialization is inevitable. The first important discovery is that after several hours the members of the test-tube groups begin to specialize and some members come to be looked up to and some to be looked down on by the others. *We have never observed a group in our studies at Minnesota where this did not happen, and no such group has been reported by other investigators.*

When it becomes clear to a person that she is specializing and when the group discovers that she is doing so, she takes a *place* in the group. She has her particular *role* in this particular group. It is the part she expects to play and the part the others expect her to play. It is indeed comparable to the concept of roles in plays, and one interesting finding of the research is that individuals change "personality" as they go from group to group. The coed who has such a sparkling personality in class and enjoys kidding around with the fellows may be quiet, devout, and reserved in her church circle. She may be ill-tempered and bossy with her family. Think of yourself. In one group you may be a take-charge person who gets things rolling. In another you are likable, joshing, and fun-loving, but not a leader at all. In a third group you are a quiet, steady, and responsible worker. Not so? Think of your first group as your own family. Your second, the people with whom you usually eat lunch. The third, you at your dorm, fraternity, sorority, or in class. Now, which is the real you? That isn't even a sensible question, really, because you change from group to group, and your personality is to some extent determined by the people around you. *The basic principle is: a member's role is worked out jointly by the person and the group.*

For this reason, also, you should not blame the group's problems on innate, unchangeable personality traits inherent in a troublesome person. Groups can be more neurotic than individuals, and they love to blame their troubles on one member — make him the scapegoat for their failures. If you understand the nature of roles and group process, you no longer will make that mistake. Instead of wishing you could get rid of Bill so you could have a decent outfit, you ask what the group is doing to Bill to make him act as he does. You begin to look for ways to change the role structure of the work group so every member can live up to his potential. You begin to utilize the entire resources of the group.

Status. Once everyone has found his place, a second important thing happens. The group judges the relative worth of each role. They give the roles they judge more valuable a higher status than the others. After a group has been working together for several hours, a trained observer can arrange the status ladder by watching the way the members talk and act. They will talk directly and more often to the people they consider important. High status people talk more to the entire group. The high status people receive more consideration from the others. The others listen to what a high status individual says; they often stop what they are doing to come to him; they stop talking to hear him, and they agree more and more emphatically with him. The group tends to ignore and cut off comments by low status members.

Struggle for status. Since much esteem and prestige reward goes to the "leader" and other high status members, several members compete for the top positions. In this competition they come into conflict; there are disagreements. The group's energy is directed to the question of who will win out, and attention is drawn away from the work. In extreme cases the struggles become heated, and the group gets bogged down. Every new group must go through a "shakedown cruise" during which the members test roles and find out who is "top dog," who is best liked, and so forth. During the "shakedown cruise," secondary tensions mount, and people who are contending for leadership come into conflict.

The basic process. How do roles emerge? How do specialization and status come about? Here is the intriguing core of what makes small groups tick. Here our research has been thorough and very fascinating. The result of our research was the discovery of the descriptive emergent model of group process we mentioned briefly in Part I. Here we explain that model in detail as it relates to role emergence. Just as individual anatomies differ from textbook diagrams, so work groups will deviate from our model; yet this, basically, is the way work group roles emerge:

Five students are placed in a test-tube group. They have not been given any role assignment; that is, no one has said that Joe will be secretary and Bill, leader. They do not know one another, and they have no reason to view any of the others as anything but equals. As a group, they do have a clear goal and a definite set of jobs that have to be done. In addition to Joe and Bill, the group contains Harry, Don, and Wilbur.

We could just as well have used an all-female group for our example because the dynamics would be the same as for an all-male group. When we have groups composed of men and women, however, several additional factors serve to complicate matters.

Sexual attractions among men and women will change the social dynamics of a group. Leadership is also complicated by the sex factor. Men tend to resist the leadership of a woman, no matter how capable, and will malinger or actively work against her efforts to structure the group's work. In recent years, with the rise of Women's Liberation, we have noticed a similar attitude on the part of some women. We have made several case studies in which two or more women members of a group have refused, as a matter of principle, to follow any plans suggested by a man. We have also noticed a greater willingness on the part of some men to allow a woman to lead a group, apparently as a result of recent concern for woman's place in society. When a group becomes a battleground for conflict between the sexes, the possibility of successful group work is slim. To keep our description of the process as basic as possible, therefore, we will use a same sex, in this case an all-male group, for our purposes.

Each of the men in our model group could do every task that is required to have the group succeed. Each, however, can do some of the things the group needs to have done better than others. Joe, for example, has been trained in technical mechanical matters. He is talented in planning and building machines. Bill is more adept at making plans for group action. He likes to divide a job into its component parts and find people to do the various tasks. Harry is good at testing ideas. The group has many different specific tasks that must be done, and to do them, they have to depend upon the resources and skills of the five members.

Remember that the work group is a social event. In addition to getting the job done, the group needs to take care of certain housekeeping chores of a social sort. Again all five could do all of the social things, but each is more skilled at some than at others.

We will begin the process of group structuring with a social concern. The members feel the typical primary tension common to the first group meeting. Don and Wilbur have been tension releasers in other groups and both have some talent in this human relations skill. They both enjoy the rewards that come from releasing social tension—the laughter, the social approval, being well liked. Generally, the person who assumes the tension-release function becomes the most popular member. Don and Wilbur are both alert to any signs of primary tension, and they find a stiff social atmosphere uncomfortable. They both must try to "break the ice." Don has his characteristic way of being funny. He begins by making small talk about anything that comes into his head. When he sees someone respond in a friendly way, he makes a mildly insulting comment and laughs to indicate it is all in fun. In addition, he has memorized a vast store of "stories," which he tells at the slightest provocation.

Wilbur also has his own style of humor. He is something of a clown and pantomimist. He is clever at doing impersonations and has an expressive face. Don begins to break the ice by making small talk and then insulting Harry. He waits for the response. He does not get a big laugh. The others may smile a bit, but their response is tentative. Don cannot tell whether they liked his sally or not. Wilbur is encouraged to give it a try, and he does a little pantomime routine. He watches to see how the others liked his little act. Again the response is halfhearted. Don tries again; Wilbur takes another turn. The others watch the two demonstrate their wares, and gradually they make up their minds as to whether Don or Wilbur should specialize in releasing tension or whether they might share the function. In the latter case, they would be affectionately referred to as a "couple of clowns."

The selection process is accomplished subconsciously. The group members are generally not aware of what is going on. They notice only that, say, Don is tactless and something of a smart aleck and that Wilbur is really pretty funny. When Harry comes to this conclusion, he begins to laugh at Wilbur and to ignore Don's attempts at humor. Then Bill and Joe may begin to see Wilbur's humor and start to laugh at him. If Don continues to insult people or tell his "old" stories, the others may begin to groan and in other ways let him know that he ought to "knock it off." After a time, Wilbur will do more and more of the tension releasing and Don will stop and move on to other functions. At this point, the struggle for the high status function of being well liked and releasing social tensions will be over. Wilbur will be a specialist. He will expect to be funny, and the group will expect him to step in when things get tense and inject a little humor to relax the atmosphere. If Wilbur fails to play his role—if he appears at a group meeting one day with a long face and is quiet and glum, the group will resent his change. Wilbur, they'll say, is not himself today. They'll ask him if he's sick. Should Wilbur try to get serious and make an important decision for the group, they will probably laugh at him.

Once the social tensions are broken, the group will go to work. Now they need someone with a "take charge" skill to step in and get them rolling. Bill and Harry have done this task for other groups, and they enjoy the rewards of being the take charge person. As soon as Harry feels that the primary tension has been released, he grows restless and wants to get down to business. He says, "All right. Let's get going. I suggest we begin by . . ." He does not get immediate obedience. The other members do not say, "That's a good idea. Let's go." They seldom even nod approval. They say little one way or another. Now Bill is encouraged to try his hand. He says, "I don't quite understand what you mean. Would you run through that again?" Harry patiently explains his plan of action, thinking to himself that Bill is not very bright. Bill now sees what Harry is driving at but says, "I'm not sure that we have to do it that way. How about this? Wouldn't this be better?" Bill now makes a suggestion of his own as to how the group might go about its work. Gradually the group begins to follow Bill's directions and orders more often than they follow Harry's. At that point, Bill will have emerged as the group's *leader.*

In much the same way, each person gradually learns that he is to specialize in certain social and task concerns. Each is led to specialize by the group's encouragement. They agree with him when he does what they want him to do, and they disagree when he does not and thus discourage him from a role they do not feel they need or will not accept him in.

A given person does not have a complete monopoly on the role functions he "ends up with," but he will carry out most of these assigned functions for the group. That is, Harry may turn out to have a wry wit which the group appreciates because it is intellectual and subtle compared to Wilbur's more physical and obvious humor, so Harry is indeed witty from time to time even though Wilbur does most of the tension releasing. In the same way, Joe may take charge of getting certain technical jobs completed even though Bill is the member who does this for the group most of the time. Although some roles are established quickly and easily, the role of *leader* is among the last to emerge. Sometimes no leader emerges at all. At Minnesota, John Geier made a careful in-depth study of sixteen such groups working together for as long as twelve weeks. Almost one-third never succeeded in having a leader emerge or in having the other roles settle down. The groups in which a leader failed to emerge were uniformly unsuccessful at their jobs and were, further-more, socially punishing to their members. They were torn with strife, they wasted much time, and they frustrated the people in them. Much of their energy went into contention for high status positions, and little was left over for productive effort. These groups suffered from absenteeism and low levels of cohesiveness.

Those groups in which a leader emerged and the roles settled down in such a pattern that every member was happy with his or her place were successful. Members of such groups knew what to expect when they came to work. They knew what they were supposed to do and how the other members of the group would react to them. They could relax and "be themselves." Typically, the test-tube groups experienced a dramatic increase in cohesiveness when the role structure became stable.

Norms. During the "shakedown cruise," as the group is developing specialized roles for its members, another process is at work creating common ways of doing things. We call these common or standard operating procedures *group norms.* Groups develop norms dealing with both the task dimension and the social interactions. Groups with clear goals will try to achieve them, and because of the response they get from other groups and organizations, they soon learn whether their work norms are successful or unsuccessful. The basketball team whose goal is to win games learns soon enough how good it is at its task. Another set of norms governs the way the members get along with one another as people. The members may adopt a common way of dressing or of wearing their hair or of talking with one another. They may even develop an unusual vocabulary when meeting as a group. Social norms are less obviously tied to achieving group goals and thus often become more unusual and bizarre than the norms related to the task.

(1) *Aping behavior.* One of the most important features of group dynamics is the power of nonverbal and verbal suggestion to get people to act as others around them are acting. "Follow-the-leader" impulses are so instinctive that we call them aping behavior because apes and monkeys often mimic the things they see other apes, monkeys, or people do.

A person stops on the street and begins to look at the sky. Soon several other people stop and look upward. When a knot of people are standing, peering towards the heavens, the impulse of someone coming upon the group to stop and do likewise is strong.

Suppose a group of students are meeting for the first time. A member confidently slouches back in his seat and puts his feet on the table. He makes an informal and slangy comment about the class and the purpose of the meeting.

Another member tips his chair back against the blackboard and agrees with the first, using the same sort of language. Several more members follow suit and soon the pressure on the one or two remaining people in the group also to assume an informal posture and use slangy speech is very strong. The group develops an informal way of gesturing and uses slangy, inside-dopester language in its discussions.

(2) *The pressure to conform and cohesiveness.* As the group develops higher levels of cohesiveness the pressure on group members to adopt the group's norms increases. The more attractive the group, the more likely the member will be to do as the group does, even though its norms are in conflict with those of other groups to which he or she belongs. Many times parents of teen-agers discover that their norms for attractive clothing or hairstyles are in conflict with those of a highly cohesive peer group, and they often lose in their attempts to influence their children's dress and hairstyle.

(3) *Overt pressure for conformity.* Members of highly cohesive groups are sensitive to failure to act as the group norms require because they often see such failure as evidence of lack of commitment to the group. They often put overt pressure on deviant members to achieve conformity to group norms. Members who see nonconformity as a threat to the group usually take steps to bring the nonconformist into line. Often they begin by talking to the member. The first comments are usually light and humorous. If the group norm is to wear dirty and obviously patched blue jeans, the members may begin to make cracks about the well-dressed member. The criticism is thus sweetened by a laugh and the release of tension that it produces.

If gentle teasing and humorous comments do not change the behavior, the communication may become more cutting and may contain ridicule and satire. Instead of laughing with the nonconformist, they now begin to laugh at him. If the member still does not conform, the others will often change from satire and ridicule to direct and serious persuasion. If the deviant member still remains a nonconformist, the others may reject him and isolate him from future communications.

(4) *Changing group norms.* The norms of a group are something like the habits of an individual. The norms may develop haphazardly, and some may be useful and productive for both task efficiency and member satisfaction. Others may be inefficient and punishing to members. Like habits, norms can be changed by accident or by plan. Groups can discuss their norms, discover their weaknesses, and by conscious effort change them.

In one student group composed of three men and two women, the women became very bored and unproductive members. When the group paused and viewed a video tape of one of their meetings and discussed the problem, they discovered that the men had developed the habit of not paying any attention to the substantive comments of the women. The men listened and responded when the women made social comments, but when the group got down to the task, they ignored the ideas of the women. As a result of the discussion of the group's do-not-listen-to-the-women norm, the men resolved to listen in the future. When they fell back into the old habits, the women reminded them of their resolve. Gradually a new and more productive norm developed, and the women became interested and productive members of the group.

Building Cohesive Groups

Cohesiveness is dynamic. To build cohesiveness for your group you need to know some of the dynamics of group process. Every member of the work group is constantly experiencing pushes into and pulls away from the group. The cohesiveness of the group fluctuates from day to day. It is one of the dynamic, changing features of groups. A unit that is highly cohesive this year — an effective, hard-hitting group — may suffer a series of reverses, change members, and lose cohesiveness so that next year it is in serious trouble.

The work group is under constant external pressures. Some of these pressures aid cohesiveness and some detract from it. If the group comes in competition with similar groups, cohesiveness is usually increased. One reason athletic teams develop such high levels of team spirit and will-to-win is that they compete with other teams in a win-or-lose situation. Coaches know the importance of cohesiveness and how to build it. On the other hand, a *competing* group may put pressure on a member to lure her away from a group and thus decrease her feeling of commitment. If you wish to examine the cohesiveness of your group, you must look to the other groups that are competing for the loyalty of the members. This is to say, the attractiveness of her group for a given person is partly dependent on the *next best group* that she could join. This becomes the comparison group. If the next best group becomes more attractive, the person may leave her present group (job) for the other group (another organization).

Make your group rewarding. If you want to know how attractive your group is to a person, total up the rewards it furnishes her, subtract the costs, and the remainder is an index of group attractiveness. A typical dictionary definition of *reward* is that it is a "recompense" that is given "for some service or attainment." A *cost* is the opposite of a reward. Rewards furnished each member by the group build cohesiveness; costs extracted from her discourage group loyalty and, if they grow too heavy, she will leave the group.

Individual motivation. To understand how a group can reward a person, we must first understand human needs and wants in general. Professor William S. Howell of the University of Minnesota, a leading authority on persuasion, points out that motives are "sources of energy" within the individual that move (motivate) him to "pursue selected alternates." Each person has a set of motives that give him the energy to move from his bed in the morning and pursue his daily activities. He could pursue a number of alternatives, but he selects the path that leads him to work with a particular group. Why one group rather than another? The answer depends upon his motivation.

Do not confuse *motivate* with *persuade*. You do not wire people with motives; they already have motives. People do things for their reasons, not yours, and you must plug into the energy already there. To persuade people, you must provide them with rewards that they find attractive because of their present needs.

Although people have very different motive structures, progress has been made in recent years toward a sensible general description of what makes people tick. Our brief outline is based on the explanations of such social scientists as A. H. Maslow and G. W. Allport and on Howell's adaptation of their work.

60

The key to this explanation of human motivation is the *sequential* arrangement of basic needs. Some needs take priority over others, and these more basic needs must be satisfied first. Only when the lower needs are satisfied can higher level needs emerge. Picturing the motives as rungs on a ladder helps visualize the priorities:

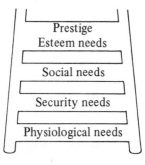

Figure 2 Deficit Ladder of Human Motivations. These motives are basic universals common to everyone, and they can be thought of as minimum essentials. A lack at any level is usually sufficient to trigger a person's energy resources and make him seek out rewards that will satisfy the need.

(1) *Physiological needs.* The first and most important rung of the ladder consists of the physiological needs – the most elementary and universal. These include such things as food, drink, activity, sleep, and sex. A thirsty person thinks of little else but drink. When she has all the water she can drink, however, other needs come to the surface. She begins to climb the ladder. The basic principle is that *unsatisfied needs are motivators of behavior.* When basic needs are satisfied and the first rung is reached, the unsatisfied needs of the next rung begin to dominate the individual's attention and actions.

(2) *Security needs.* We want to be secure – to have a predictable and organized life. We want to look into the future and know pretty well what will happen.

(3) *Social needs.* When the need for security is largely filled, the social needs begin to dominate. These are extremely important in developing a cohesive work group because they are the needs the group is uniquely equipped to gratify. They

include the need to belong to a group and to give and receive acceptance.

(4) *Status and esteem needs.* When the social needs are satisfied, the desire for status and esteem becomes dominant. We need to feel that we stand high in the eyes of others. We want a good reputation and position. We need prestige. Associated with the need for prestige is the desire for esteem. There are two sides to this motive — a public and a private side. The public side is that we need to be highly regarded by others. We need recognition, respect, and appreciation. This is not the same as status. For example, we gain status because of our reputation or because we inherited wealth, no matter what kind of person we are. Esteem is earned by our association with others. The private side is that we need to like ourselves. We want to feel self-confident, to have a good image of ourselves, and to feel that we really are important. Members of affluent societies often find their physiological and security needs largely satisfied, but they seldom have all of the status and esteem they want. Most of us are struggling to climb the upper rungs of the deficit ladder. Here is where work groups can provide some of their most powerful rewards.

(5) *Unselfishness.* The deficit ladder includes only the selfish motives — needs closely related to preserving our individual self and gratifying our ego. We look to these motives when we are out for "number one." We must always remember, however, that people often act unselfishly. They go out of their way to help others; they deny their own status to raise the status of others; they make personal sacrifices for the good of the group.

(6) *The desire to work.* The deficit ladder does not account for the drive to work. The notion that individuals are essentially mean, lazy, slothful, and want only to avoid work is a holdover from an old theological view of man. Recent social science and medical research indicate that we need and seek out work. The drive for workmanship is so strong that if it is frustrated on the day-to-day job, the individual will develop hobbies that give it release. He will have a home workshop,

remodel his house, or landscape his yard. Psychiatrist Karl Menninger judges that "we must work in order to live . . ." Indeed, occupational therapy — giving the patient work that he can do — is an integral part of psychiatric treatment. People do not have to be coerced, goaded, and forced to work for a group. They will seek out opportunities to do worthwhile and satisfying labor. An influential contemporary expert on management, Douglas McGregor, advocates *achievement* reward as the key to modern management.

Group rewards. Groups can furnish rewards at each rung of the deficit ladder. Insofar as your group furnishes you with more rewards more abundantly than the next best group you could join, you will find it attractive and you will work for the group.

(1) *Material rewards.* The work group may give a member material rewards. It may give him a salary, bonuses, or other cash benefits. Money can satisfy a number of motives; certainly it buys the things that fulfill the basic physiological needs—food, drink, shelter, and health care.

The group may also give a member indirect material benefits. Other members may help him make business contacts. Becoming a member of the country club may increase an insurance broker's sales.

However, just as the group may satisfy basic physiological needs, it may frustrate them. A member may make less money by staying with a particular group. He may receive fewer fringe benefits, sell less insurance, or even lose business because of his association. When this happens, the group's attraction is weakened.

The pull of cold cash offered by a given group is a function of the next best offer. If his present group pays him $8,000 per year and the next best job has a salary of $5,000, a member will find his present group much more attractive than if the next best offer is $7,500. Of course, if the offer is $9,000, the present group will begin to cost him. He may remain with his present group because it gives him other rewards, but he will not be as strongly drawn as he was when the group was giving him superior monetary rewards.

When a leader seeks to hire a person from another group,

she often thinks first of offering more material rewards to appeal to that person's physiological needs. She suggests an increase in salary, greater fringe benefits, and perhaps more money in the future.

The leader of a group may use money to encourage greater effort in behalf of the group. She may give salary increases or bonuses as incentives for meeting individual quotas or for doing an outstanding job. The physiological needs are basic and appeals to them are effective; their continued use testifies to that.

However, when the basic physiological needs are met, a person no longer works for them. More money at this stage will do little to make a person work harder or be more loyal to the group. Douglas McGregor makes the point strongly in his new approach to management; he suggests that money may be a dissatisfier in that a person who feels he or she deserves more (is worth more) than he or she gets will be dissatisfied. In this case, money does not serve as a reward to greater effort.

Money is an obvious reward, but it is mentioned here only to lay the groundwork for the less obvious ones.

(2) *Security rewards.* The group can provide its members with security. Money, of course, can also purchase insurance policies, mutual funds, and retirement annuities to give security. In addition, if the group has established ways of meeting and working, it provides the individual with a secure social environment. A person knows what to expect when working with other members of the group and finds such security rewarding.

(3) *Social rewards.* The group can provide its members with powerful social rewards. It can make a person feel that she belongs. Our psychiatrists, novelists, and playwrights continually emphasize the role of loneliness in mental disturbances. A work group can provide an individual with contacts with other people who know her as a person and like and respect her. In one of the groups studied at the University of Minnesota, where classes can be very large and commuting students absorbed in their own busy lives, a

foreign student said that, for the first time in his two years in this country, he had gotten to know some American students and to make some real friends. He found this fully as important to him as the work satisfactions and material rewards he received.

On the other hand, the group can be socially punishing. The social relations may be in a constant flux. The individual never knows for sure what is expected and may feel rejected. The group may treat the person as someone of little worth. When this happens, the individual may leave the group.

(4) *Prestige rewards.* The work group can provide its members with prestige rewards. When a group develops a good reputation, it sheds its prestige on all the members, thus increasing a person's reputation in the community. The individual will boast of membership in an elite organization and may even wear some public sign of membership, such as a pin, a ring, or a special piece of clothing.

Conversely, the group may have a bad reputation, perhaps from having unsavory characters as members or from an extended string of failures. The high school gang with members who have a police record or the ball team that is the conference doormat—these groups award their members little prestige.

Groups have a spongelike ability to absorb the prestige of their members. The group's reputation is enhanced when important people join. Voluntary organizations quite often print the names of famous and prestigious members on a letterhead. Work groups also develop a reputation in their own right. They gain prestige by doing a good job. Among production units, the one with the highest output of quality goods is the "best."

However, the prestige of a group is seldom constant. The group's efficiency depends on its cohesiveness, which tends to fluctuate in cycles. Cohesiveness grows and yields greater productivity, which increases the prestige of the group, which increases the cohesiveness, which results in still greater task efficiency. Should this upward spiral be broken, the downward slide can begin. A change in personnel, a failure of some size, a loss of prestige (the public often likes to see the top dog stumble), will decrease cohesiveness, which will further impair task efficiency, and the downward spiral begins. Good groups must always be on guard to keep overconfidence and complacency from starting the downward cycle.

(5) *Esteem rewards.* The group can provide its members with esteem rewards. If an individual becomes important within the group—if he emerges as a leader, is well respected, well liked, looked up to—he will receive esteem rewards. Time and time again a person who is given prestigeful work within the group, who does a good job, and who is recognized as an important and worthwhile worker, becomes more strongly drawn to his unit.

The work group may also deprive a person of her esteem needs. If the others make it clear to her that she is unimportant to them, they deprive her of her esteem needs. She will need a great deal of money or other reward to make up for such deprivation. Much of the nonparticipation, the so-called "dead wood" in organizations and work groups, results from this factor. Highly cohesive groups make every person feel that she is important to the team, a worthy individual doing her share—even though she does not speak up or do other than routine chores. The others, *at the very least,* assure her that they esteem her as a person and a fellow worker.

(6) *Work rewards.* The group can provide its members with work rewards, work satisfactions. The group can satisfy the instinct for workmanship in two ways. First, it may provide a person with an opportunity to do the kind of work he likes to do. A person's vocational choice is closely tied to his ultimate happiness and satisfaction. Some groups will provide an individual with the chance to do exciting and significant things. He may sacrifice some monetary rewards and prestige and esteem satisfactions if he is doing the job he loves to do. Second, the group provides him with other people who can appreciate a good job. Even when we know that we have done an excellent piece of work, we do not get maximum satisfaction until other people, whose opinion we respect, honestly and sincerely appreciate the job.

These work and esteem needs are often met in leadership positions. At the very time when the people working at menial jobs, jobs that provide few if any of these satisfactions, are demanding shorter hours, the managers work long hours above and beyond what is required. The higher the level of leadership, the greater the effort. The increase in commitment and dedication on the part of leaders in all kinds of groups is a function of the increased work and esteem satisfactions.

The work group can deprive its members of work satisfactions, also. The worker may be required to do tasks he finds dull or unchallenging. The family may require the mother to wash diapers, wipe runny noses, and scrub floors. If she finds such work unrewarding and unappreciated, she will find it distasteful to do or she may fail to do it at all. The highly cohesive groups studied at the University of Minnesota all developed ways in which the entire group (not just the leader) made it clear to a person that they appreciated the work he had done when he did a particularly good job. Even if someone enjoys his work and feels he is doing it well, he will become disgruntled if no one notices his efforts. As we said, people are not inherently lazy, but we do have to feel that what we are doing is important and, further, that what we are doing is appreciated.

(7) *Losing the self in a cause.* Some special groups generate cohesiveness by working for a good cause. Groups dedicated to religious and spiritual objectives or to causes may become highly cohesive. Many of today's social movements, such as Women's Liberation and Gay Liberation, also provide their members with the rewards that come from working for a cause.

Such groups provide an opportunity for the individual to transcend the self and find a larger meaning in life. People who join an organization and fight for a cause believe they are taking positive action. They feel they are having an effect on their community and country. Rewards of this type can create a level of commitment that exceeds any that result from appeals to the selfish motives on the deficit ladder.

History is filled with examples of individuals who chose to give their lives fighting for a cause. People who feel they have a responsibility to make the world a better place often feel guilty if they do not take action. A group dedicated to a cause can assuage these guilt feelings. The group should spell out clearly its basic beliefs and reiterate them for all new members. Frequent statements of the group's purpose, clearly and forcibly put, will assure that everyone understands the common goals.

Group attraction for the individual. At any given moment, an individual feels the pull of his group because it satisfies one or more of his basic needs. He is pushed from the organization if he finds that one or more of these needs will never be met. In addition, his loyalty is determined by the *relative deprivation* he feels at each rung of the ladder. The man with inherited wealth may keep a low-paying professorship at a small college because he enjoys his job, while a poor man would move to a better-paying school. Likewise, if one group fails to satisfy a person's need for esteem, but he has other ways to gain these rewards from groups such as the family, church, or Boy Scouts, he may still remain loyal to this group because it enables him to meet his need for workmanship or fighting for a cause.

Clearly, if you understand the way a group can satisfy the motivations of its members, you are well on the way to understanding the *process* by which cohesiveness is generated within the group. The group member or leader who understands this process can really apply the advice that he or she should build the most highly cohesive group possible.

Group interaction builds cohesion. To this point we have been examining cohesiveness in terms of the total group attractiveness to each individual member. As all of the members interact during their meetings, they also generate powerful forces for cohesion.

(1) *Group fantasy chains.* One important way in which groups develop common ground among the members is by joking and talking about things that do not always have to do with the business at hand. If we watch a group that is working along quite well, they sometimes come to a point where they stumble and seem to lose the thread of the discussion. They

are unable to get back on the track. The members slump down in their chairs, begin to fiddle with their papers or pencils, look bored. The talk dribbles off, and there are long pauses.

Then one member says something completely off the subject about some person who is not part of the meeting or about somebody he has read about or seen on TV or about something that has happened to him recently or about something he wishes would happen to him in the future. Another member responds with a laugh and adds onto the story. Another member joins in and soon the entire group comes alive. They all begin talking, and they grow emotional. They may laugh or express fear or sadness. Then, as abruptly as it started, the episode is broken off by someone who usually pulls the group back to work.

We call these moments of dramatization which excite the group members and in which all or most of them participate *group fantasy chains.* You should not get the impression we are using the term *fantasy* in the sense that the communication is like science fiction or like a fairy story. A group fantasy may deal with real-life situations and people. We mean by fantasy that the situation is removed from the here-and-now reality of the group, and the people in the episode are not acting in the presence of the group members at this particular time.

The group fantasy chain works something like the dreams that we have as individuals. When we daydream about people we admire doing things we would like to do or when we see ourselves acting out things we would like to do, we reveal our values, our goals, and our motives. If someone knows our most intimate daydreams, she can tell a good deal about how we will act.

Group fantasy chains serve to create common dreams for a group of people and thus build common ground for future decisions. For example, suppose we set up a group of five college students and give them a task to do for a class. The students start to work and soon discover some difference of opinion as to how they should go about their job. They also discover that one member is very task-oriented and wants things to be carefully organized and another is rather carefree and keeps suggesting that the group make sure that no member has to spend too much time in the library. The talk begins to die out. Somebody mentions an upcoming social event on campus. There is a pause and the task-oriented member tries to bring the group back to the job at hand. The carefree member says in a joking way, "Oh, you're just like my father." Another member picks it up. "Really, what do you mean?" "My father is always driving us to get work done around the house. You can't take off a minute, and he comes around with a hammer or a paint brush or something." The group members begin to chime in with responses to an authority figure who is a taskmaster and with other examples of their own relating to similar characters and similar events.

In the course of chaining out the fantasy, they build a common ground about the style of leadership they prefer and their attitudes towards working for the group. Should the general attitude developed in the fantasy chain be negative towards authority figures who are constantly driving people to work, the taskmaster will undoubtedly not emerge as the leader of this particular group.

When groups chain out a number of fantasies of this sort over a period of time, they build a group culture, and they often allude to the heroes and villains of their fantasy chains as they interact with one another.

(2) *Group reminiscences.* Group fantasies tend to be remembered because they are always accompanied by high feelings, emotions, and excitement. Other events occur to the group which impress themselves on the members and which they recall in their discussions.

On one occasion a student group was meeting in the evening in a campus building. One member had to come late and found the building locked. The resulting problems and the final solution caused considerable excitement for the group, and they often remembered the event when reminiscing about their common experiences. Whenever a group develops inside jokes or nicknames resulting from fantasy themes that they have chained out or from unusual happenings or adventures, they begin to feel part of an identifiable group.

(3) *Group rites and rituals.* Sometimes the group will do things related to their fantasies and their history over and over again until they take on the characteristics of rites and rituals. Repeating the action makes the past experience live again to some extent. One student group was in the process of developing cohesion and finding places for the members in the group's role structure when a member pulled a candy bar out of her purse and offered to share it with the rest. Another member in a clowning mood took out a penknife and made something of an event out of cutting the candy equally and sharing fairly. Subsequently, some member always brought some food to the meeting, and it was always cut into equal portions by the same penknife and eaten before the members got down to business.

Seven Concrete Steps to Greater Cohesiveness for Your Work Group

Identify your group. Mention your group as a group. Talk about *we, our* group, what *we* hope to accomplish, and how *we* can continue *our* excellent work. Do not accentuate the *I*. The leader should not continually stress such things as, "I want this done," or "I'm asking you to do this as a personal favor to me," or "If you don't do this, I'll find it necessary to. . ." Highly cohesive groups also always work out ways to identify their group; sometimes these are as obvious as insignia, or mascots, or the use of nicknames.

Build a group tradition. No sooner is a group clearly identified than things happen to it. Fantasies chain out and are remembered. The unit begins to have a history. Unusual, exciting, or funny things can become a part of its history and tradition. The leader can build cohesiveness by recalling these events in group meetings because such recollections emphasize the fact that the group exists through time. Highly cohesive work groups have traditional events or ceremonies that give the unit added meaning and build loyalty. Highly cohesive families have such traditions that help them celebrate certain holidays or special occasions in the family's history.

Stress teamwork. Accept the basic principle of professional athletic teams. Simply put, it is: I don't care if I star so long as we win. Television sportscasters interviewing a home-run hitter will often ask, "How many home runs are you going to hit this year?" A good team player always replies, "I don't care just so long as we win the pennant." Don't worry about who gets the credit so long as your group succeeds.

Get the group to recognize good work. Encourage the group to fulfill the social and esteem needs of one another. The leader can watch the group for compliments being paid, offers to help each other with outside projects, and even the simple social recognition of a member by offers of a ride home or invitations to coffee. When these occur, the wise participant or leader will encourage them and add a compliment, always praising work in terms of the importance of the contribution to the group. Too often, the leader becomes pre-occupied with the high status members, but it is the quiet, non-participating member who has the greatest need for social and esteem rewards. Too often the attention paid to the low status member is negative. Criticism of his lack of interest, or knowledge, or partici-pation will only make matters worse. A little positive attention to the marginal individual, the potential "dead wood," will go a long way toward increasing group cohesiveness.

Set clear, attainable group goals. Your work group may have some general long-term goals, but a goal several months in the future is too vague for building cohesiveness. A goal for a given meeting, for this week, for next week, is much more likely to increase morale. Achieving a goal rewards the group. Making daily or weekly progress provides such rewards regularly. Of course, if the goal is to be useful, it must be clearly specified and understood by all, and *it must be within reach.* The miler who sees the finish line and thinks he can catch the leader puts on a burst of speed.

Give group rewards. Reaching a clear goal is a group reward in itself, but the leader or supervisor can emphasize the identity of the group, help build a tradition, and stress teamwork by giving the *entire* group a common reward for achieving a goal. Too many organizations have geared their *entire* incentive system to the old view of managing individuals. Individual incentives have been stressed over group incentives. If a coach encouraged every player to be a star — to look out only for himself and cut down every other person on his team — that coach would be in trouble. That team would be in trouble.

One need not give up individual incentives to make wise use of group rewards. These may be monetary or they may be rewards aimed at the needs for esteem and workmanship. Letters of commendation for the group, plaques, dinners, or other social affairs in recognition of a group job well done, these all help.

If a leader or supervisor receives personal recognition, such as a special award or letter of commendation, he or she should call a meeting of the group and reflect this recognition back on them. The old, "I could not have done it without each and every one of you" speech is given so often because it is important to the cohesiveness of the group and because it is, simply, true.

Treat members like people, not machines. The clean precision and absolute efficiency of a highly tooled machine is often taken as the ideal for the workings of a group or the conduct of a meeting. Many organizations would function much more smoothly if the people in them were standard, replaceable, predictable parts such as those that fit in our mass-produced automobiles. People trained in science and technology often try to work with groups as they work with machines. When they do, the situation often explodes in their faces. Frequently they respond by charging that others are unreasonable, because a sensible blueprint for action has been rejected or sabotaged. Human response is difficult to predict. People are not computers. Several decades ago time-and-motion-study engineers developed much more efficient by-the-numbers ways of doing routine jobs. When they tried to get people to adopt these new ways, the workers resisted, and the result was not greater efficiency but less. One large cause of wasted time and inefficiency in the modern organization is the feeling of many of its members that they are cogs in a large and inhuman machine and that nobody recognizes them as human beings who amount to something.

Building a Positive Social Climate

When a new work group starts. In this section we are going to deal with the principles of getting a committee meeting, business conference, or discussion group off on the right foot. These principles can also be used in dealing with more permanent groups, but they are easier to study in newly formed units.

When the members of a new group meet for the first time, they begin to interact socially. They nod or talk to one another. They smile, frown, and laugh. All of these things help build a climate that is pleasant, congenial, and relaxed, or one that is cold, stiff, and tense. A positive social climate makes for an attractive group; it builds cohesiveness by providing social rewards, and it encourages people to speak up and say what they really mean.

Professor Robert Bales and his associates at Harvard University have determined that three types of concrete actions build a good social feeling and three opposite actions build a negative climate. Our discussion is based upon the research from Harvard with modifications from our own research at the University of Minnesota. The positive actions are shows of solidarity, tension release, and agreement. The negative actions are shows of antagonism, tension, and disagreement.

Show solidarity. Any action or statement that indicates to the others that the new group is important is a show of solidarity. Raising another's status, offering to help do something for the group, volunteering, or indicating you are willing to go out of your way and make a personal sacrifice for the group shows solidarity.

The negative side to solidarity is to show antagonism to the group or to another person. While shows of solidarity build a pleasant spirit and rapport, shows of antagonism make the others uncomfortable.

Deal with social tensions. People in new groups always feel a certain amount of tension. Feelings of embarrassment, shyness, and uneasiness when meeting strangers are shows of social tension.

(1) *Primary tensions.* When the discussion group first meets, everyone will experience *primary* tensions. They feel ill at ease. They do not know what to say or how to begin. The first meeting is tense and cold and must be warmed up. When groups experience primary tension, the people speak very softly; they sigh, and they are very polite. They seem bored and uninterested. No person is really bored when she has an opportunity to speak up and make a name for herself. However, every individual gambles a great deal by plunging into the meeting, by taking an active part. She may make a good showing. The others may be impressed by her ability and decide they like her as a person, *but* they may be

irritated by her. They may decide she is stupid and un-informed; they may reject her. This gamble makes a person feel nervous and tense, and she may take flight from the situation by pretending she is not interested. Do not be misled. The person who seems bored and uninterested is really very tense and most interested, particularly in the social dimension of the group. If the meeting never releases the primary tension, the whole style of future meetings may be set in this uncomfortable mold. It is vital that the primary tension be released early! Tension is released through indications of pleasure such as smiles, chuckles, and laughs. Spend some time joking and socializing before getting down to business. Judiciously used, a bit of socializing is time wisely spent. Once the primary tension is released, however, the group should go to work. Waiting too long to get started will waste time. The leader should develop a sense of timing so that she will know when to stop chatting and get on with the job.

(2) *Secondary tensions.* Once people relax and get down to work, new and different social tensions are generated by role struggles, disagreements over ideas, and personality conflicts. Secondary tensions are louder than primary ones. People speak rapidly, they interrupt one another, are impatient to get the floor and have their say; they may get up and pace the room or pound the table. When secondary tensions reach a certain level, the group finds it difficult to concentrate on its job. When that point is reached, the tensions should be released by humor, direct comment, or conciliation. Secondary tensions are more difficult to bleed off than primary ones. There are no easy solutions, but they should not be ignored! By all means, bring them out into the open and talk them over.

Show agreement. Agreement is one of the basic social rewards. Agreements are like money in the bank that buys social status and esteem rewards. When the group agrees with a member, they tender her social currency. They say: we value you. When the others agree with us, we lose our primary tension; we loosen up; we get excited;

we take a more active part in the meeting. The more people agree, the more they communicate with one another.

Disagreements serve as negative climate builders. When people disagree, they grow cautious and tense. *Disagreements are socially punishing but absolutely essential to good group work.* They are double-edged. They are necessary to sound thinking. Yet, disagreements always contain an element of personal attack. The person who finds her ideas subjected to rigorous testing and disagreement feels like she is being "shot down."

Successful discussion groups studied at Minnesota worked out ways to tolerate and even encourage disagreements. *None of them, however, managed to keep the disagreements from straining the social fabric.* One of the reasons that the number of disagreements goes up with a rise in cohesiveness is that groups must develop enough cohesiveness to afford disagreements and still not break up. The rate of disagreements is often highest in the family — the most cohesive unit in our society. How often someone complains, "You're so much nicer with strangers than with the members of your own family!"

Some people try to cushion the hurt in a disagreement by saying things like, "That's a good idea, BUT . . .", or, "That's right. I agree with you, BUT . . ." Eventually the others discover that these prefatory agreements or compliments are just ways of setting them up for the knife. They begin to cringe as the ". . . BUT I think we ought to look at the other side of it . . ." hits them. The fact is, *a disagreement, to do its job, must be perceived as a disagreement.* Disagreements are the scalpels the group uses to cut out undesirable ideas, faulty reasoning, and poor evidence. They must be understood to mean: *stop, this will not do.* When they are thus understood, no amount of kind words of introduction will serve to sugarcoat them.

Develop ways to encourage and tolerate disagreements. First, build cohesiveness. Second, do things to knit the group back together after a period of heavy disagreement. Often disagreements increase as the group moves toward a decision. Good groups have built cohesiveness to tolerate and encourage such disagreements, and they use the positive climate builders to knit the group back together after the decision is reached. They joke and laugh. They show solidarity. They say, "It was a good meeting," "It accomplished something," and,

"Let's all get behind this decision." They compliment the persons who advocated the rejected plan. They tell them they are needed, that the group cannot succeed without their help.

Another technique sometimes used by successful work groups is to make one person the "disagreer." He tests most of the ideas, and the group expects him to do so. Whenever they feel the need for disagreement, they turn to him. They reward him by giving him a nickname or by joshing him about how disagreeable he is. If a new person joins the group and asks another after the meeting, "What's with him? He's sure disagreeable," the other member would say, "Oh, don't mind Joe. He's just that way. He doesn't mean any harm. He's really a good guy; he just disagrees with everything." Since Joe plays the role of the person who always disagrees, someone finding his ideas under attack from Joe would be less hurt than he would be under the usual conditions. After all, Joe disagrees with everybody and means no harm.

Conflict Management in the Small Group

Much of our discussion of disagreements and their effect on the social fabric of the group applies to those differences among members which cause extremely high secondary tensions. The way good groups manage disagreements productively is instructive in terms of how they deal with high tension problems. Still, good groups can deal with the run-of-the-mill disagreements without too much difficulty by using their techniques for knitting the group back together and for rebuilding their social fabric. The extreme cases generally require special attention and treatment. Here we deal with conflicts, those disagreements that cause such high secondary tension as to render the group inoperative.

Conflict management in the social area. Some communication styles and contexts put people into competitive conflict. Group meetings with rules like a poker game—where a certain amount of value goes into the game but is divided unequally as a result of the communication process that takes place during the session—will bring the members into competition, and conflict will often result. In Part IV we will discuss competitive group climates such as the negotiation session, where several parties with different and conflicting goals get together to strike a bargain. The task-oriented small group in the message communication style, however, should be a cooperative meeting in which the members work together to achieve high fidelity communication by willingly playing roles of source and receiver and by providing honest feedback to aid in overcoming confusion. The task-oriented small group is also designed to achieve a common goal. Such groups generally assume that by working together, they will create value which all members can then share. They are in the same boat and will sink or succeed together.

Some group contexts (and some games) are a mixture of cooperation and competition in that, by staying together and cooperating, the members achieve greater value than they could by working separately, but the group distributes the rewards unequally. Such mixed-motive situations result in conflict as well as cohesiveness.

Although much about the task-oriented small group is cooperative, it tends, in fact, to be a mixed-motive communication climate. The conflicts in a task-oriented small group are more likely to arise from the dynamics of the role structuring than from task discussion. The amount of value earned by productive work may grow and all may share in task success, but the internal social rewards are distributed unequally as some members grow in status, influence, and attractiveness, while others sink into lower status, less influence, and less popularity.

The conflicts arise from the three major areas of social rewards. The emergence of leadership is a prime source of interpersonal conflict among members. Those individuals who remain as potential leaders after the group eliminates the obviously unsuitable will often come into conflict. The way some members acquire influence in the task dimension and assume exciting and interesting task assignments while others are encouraged to take on routine tasks often results in apathy on the part of the low status members, in clique formation, and, on occasion, in actual efforts at sabotage of the group's work out of frustration because of unsatisfactory rewards in relation to other members. The way members come to be well liked and popular is still another source of conflict. Less socially rewarded members may become jealous.

Groups often find conflicts in the social dimension difficult to deal with. Social conflicts result in defensive communication as discussed in Part I. When interpersonal conflict erupts, the level of secondary tension shoots up to destructive levels. Member discomfort is often so high that the group takes flight from the conflict.

The most common and destructive way groups take flight from conflicts in the social dimension is to ignore them. Groups often take flight into the task dimension. Since the group is task-oriented, the members can, in good conscience, ignore their social conflicts by doggedly sticking to task discussions *even though their secondary tensions have reached such levels that they cannot work effectively.* In our classroom groups we often stop the meetings periodically to discuss group process. Many unsuccessful groups report that "We were so task-oriented that we couldn't get anything accomplished." What they mean is that when social conflicts arose, instead of dealing with them, they took flight into the task area and discovered that unresolved social dimension conflicts crippled their ability to work. Groups taking flight from social conflict into dogged discussion of task topics generally conduct very tense meetings. They exhibit little tension-releasing communication. They seldom chain into fantasy themes. They do not disclose information about themselves. They do not joke around or laugh much.

When groups ignore social conflicts during formal meetings, the members often discuss their frustrations with one another in subgroups. Such discussions behind the group's back, as it were, seldom solve the difficulties. Generally, as long as the conflict is a hidden agenda item it remains a destructive force.

Another common way that groups take flight from conflicts in the social dimension is by smoothing over the difficulty. When a group smooths over a conflict the members mention the difficulty and begin to deal with it. Since the secondary tension is already high, however, opening a discussion of the sore spot causes great discomfort and the members may pull back by agreeing that they all feel much better now that the problem is "out in the open," or that having mentioned it, the problem is now solved, or that upon examining the problem, they discover it is much less severe than they had thought and probably is really no problem at all.

A basic strategy that members use to smooth a conflict is to fail to express their perceptions and feelings honestly when the subject is brought up in the meeting. Usually the member simply remains quiet and seems interested but noncommittal. Sometimes the member will physically move back a bit, away from the circle of the group, seeming to suggest nonverbally that he or she is becoming an observer rather than a participant. If someone asks a direct question, the member will deny his feelings and perceptions or play down their intensity. If the group is in the second phase of leadership emergence and the two contenders have come into conflict, the group may deny that a conflict exists by agreeing that they are "all leaders," or that they "do not need to have a leader," or that they can "all take turns being leader."

Difficult as it is for groups to discuss leadership, they often find it more difficult to discuss such matters as the influence of personal attraction, gender, and sex. They prefer to pretend to ignore the like-dislike relationships that are evolving, the influence of gender on the members' response to potential leaders and task influentials, and the influence of sexual attraction as revealed by nonverbal courtship or seduction routines.

As a general rule, the leadership, influence, achievement, and gender conflicts need to be dealt with in order for the group to continue working productively. The sexual relationships and the like-dislike patterns may be ignored or smoothed without a crippling effect. Members of work groups do not need to like one another in order to cooperate and work productively together, but they do need to evolve productive and stable role relationships.

The best technique for the management of conflict in the social dimension of the task-oriented small group is to confront the problem and work it out. The group should put the conflict on its agenda, devote sufficient time to its consideration to work it through, and pull itself back to the discussion of the conflict whenever it begins to take flight. Of course the group will have to pull back from time to time to release tension and change the subject sometimes simply to allow members to relax, or they will not be able to continue. But such withdrawal must be allowed with the knowledge that the group will return, after the change of pace, to continue to focus on and work through their conflict. To fail to face social conflicts which are crippling a task-oriented group is to leave the group permanently disabled.

In a number of ways, confrontation of social conflict in the task-oriented group resembles communication in the relationship style. The group must achieve a level of cohesiveness such that they can tolerate the tensions required to bring the conflict into the open.

They must also create a climate where members can honestly express their feelings and perceptions relating to the conflict. In one crucial respect, however, the session to confront and work through conflict in the social dimension of task groups differs from the sensitivity or encounter group meeting, and the distinction is an important one. In the relationship communication meeting the focus is upon the individual's self-image, change, growth, increased awareness and actualization, or upon relationships among individuals. In working through social conflict in the task-oriented small group, the focus should *be upon the group.*

One of the more subtle ways in which groups take flight from working through their conflicts is to explain away their difficulties as being caused by forces or persons beyond their control. They may argue, for example, that some external pressure, or some accidental occurrence, or some unreasonable demands made by an individual outside the group caused their conflict. In a classroom group students may argue that the illness and absence of a member, or lack of time, or the unreasonable demands of the instructor caused their problems. One of the most destructive ways to take flight is to select one or two members and make them the scapegoats for the conflict. The group in conflict often finds it comforting to point to bull-headed, unreasonable member "Joe," who has single-handedly sabotaged the group. Usually the flight-taking includes the explanation that Joe acted destructively because he has certain unchangeable personality traits which are thus beyond the power of the group to deal with. Under the circumstances, nothing can be done short of kicking Joe out of the group. By scapegoating, the other members can then get rid of their frustrations and guilt feelings by projecting them upon Joe.

Since scapegoating a member is a common neurotic tendency of groups in conflict, a productive confrontation session requires that the group must *under no circumstances allow its session to degenerate into cattiness or personalities.* The group must keep its focus *on the group* and the way in which role conflicts or status differences or achievement rewards are evolving, or upon norms which are destructive to a sound social dimension. The proper way to approach such conflict management is to remember that any person's behavior in a group is a joint enterprise worked out by the member and the group together. Whatever Joe's personality might be in social isolation, his role behavior as exhibited in the group is a function of that personality *and* the way the group rewards and punishes his attempts to find a role in the group. The question should always be, therefore: What is the group doing to Joe to make him act that way? rather than, What are the basic unchangeable miserable personality characteristics in Joe that result in his destruction of our group? Groups that work through their conflicts in this manner often discover that Joe is a good deal easier to work with than they thought and finally they may even come to like "good old Joe."

Some good questions to guide the group that finds itself needing conflict management in the social dimension are: Do we have stable roles? If not, are we in the final stages of leadership emergence? Who are the remaining contenders for leadership? Are we ready to announce publicly that for most of us a leader has now emerged? (Often a public avowal of leadership releases a great deal of tension and allows the person who has emerged to relax and perform the leadership-role functions with security. Once the question of leadership is symbolically settled, the others in the group can concentrate on their own roles.) Are the apathetic or less interested members turned off because a few people are doing all of the interesting and exciting things? Are the norms governing informal channels of communication such that some members seldom get the floor and when they do speak the others ignore their suggestions and ideas? Are the problems a function of gender? Are one or more of the leader contenders female and are the males (or other females) finding it difficult to take directions and orders from a female? Are the females becoming a power center because of industrious gathering of information? Does the female power center cause apathy on the part of the males? Are females disturbed because they feel that, despite talent and ability, they are not given roles that match their contributions?

Confrontation of conflict and working through to more productive and less tense social climates are encouraged in the task-oriented group because cooperation is rewarding. The group that works like a team and has high *esprit de corps* tends to be successful and fun to work with. If the members can keep their common goals before the group continually and remember the rewards of cooperative effort, the forces for cohesiveness can help in conflict resolution.

One final word of warning. When a zero-history test-tube group first tries to confront a conflict in the social dimension, the success or failure of the effort becomes a very important precedent for the future success or failure of the group. If the group should probe the conflict, raise tensions, take flight, and fail to work the problem through, then that failure is taped into their history. When the next conflict arises, the members will find it more difficult to deal with directly. If they fail a second time, then they may not deal with other conflicts at all. On the other hand, if the first confrontation is successful, the members will find it easier to deal with future conflicts, and conflicts are inevitable. A second success begins to establish a healthy norm for dealing with conflicts in the social dimension and gradually the group sees itself as a social system which knows how to handle conflict. The members are able to work through social conflicts at the appropriate times and thus free much more of the group's energy for productive task effort.

Conflict management in the task area. While conflicts are more likely in the social dimension of group interaction, they are not uncommon in the task dimension. One of the difficulties in resolving conflicts in general is that you cannot always tell from the content of the communication whether the conflict is a task disagreement or, actually, a problem in the social area. Often members in conflict over roles or in a power struggle will wage a battle over what appears to be some task issue. People may view the fate of their suggestions and ideas as evidence of their own status in the group. Reject my idea and you have rejected me, is their attitude. Or a member may gleefully report that the group has accepted (him) his or her plan of action. Sometimes a member says that it was "my idea and the group liked it." On the other hand, a member may be very upset and report that his idea was rejected by the group only to have the group accept the same idea, or a very similar one, when it was introduced by someone else later on. Very probably there is always a mixture of social status, control, and achievement involved in every task conflict. Still, task-oriented small groups do deal with important substantive matters and many conflicts are primarily related to the group's work. Groups often get feedback from the external environment indicating how well they are doing. An athletic team wins or loses games. A task force has its report accepted and praised or rejected and ignored. A business unit thrives and makes a profit or begins to lose money. A discussion group in class puts on a program and the audience likes it or is bored by it. Feedback causes the group to evaluate its work norms and decisions, and the importance of doing a good job often results in conflicts which are largely substantive. Group members should, however, analyze the nature of the conflict before attempting to resolve it. If the argument over the task issues is really a power struggle, then the group which assumes the conflict is over substantive differences may find itself taking flight into the task dimension and fail to deal with the real source of its difficulty.

Interestingly enough, groups may take flight from task conflict into the social dimension. Generally groups which take flight into socializing have very pleasant social relations. The members like one another and have built good relationships. The minute they begin to work on a common task, however, they come into conflict. Instead of fighting through the disagreements to some task consensus, they make a decision quickly, and members who do not like the decision do not disagree; they "go along." Members of such groups report "pseudo-agreement because I did not want to cause trouble." Members assert that they do not want to make waves or that "we have such a cohesive group we didn't want to hurt our cohesiveness by getting into an argument about the task." Of course, members who talk of cohesiveness in terms of dodging disagreements because they strained their sociability do not truly understand the concept of cohesiveness as we explained it earlier in this section. *Members of cohesive groups* are tightly drawn to the group and *can tolerate more disagreement and conflict* than can members of groups with low cohesiveness. Groups that must take flight from task conflict into socializing are not very cohesive at all. Cohesive groups handle the task and social dimensions of their group life with equal success.

Some task conflicts relate to work norms and procedures. The group should deal with task conflict related to matters of standard operating procedures much as it would with a conflict in the social dimension. Members may come into conflict because of differing expectations as to the satisfactory level. of task achievement. In classroom groups members may differ as to how much "work" they should do individually and as a group in order to feel good about the group product. How much outside time should members put into the group effort? How much research? People with high standards may work hard and become frustrated because others seem lazy or less hard-working. People with lower standards may be irritated by the model of the hard-working members and feel guilty because they do not do as much; yet they may be defensive about their position. Feeling both defensive and guilty, the members with lower expectations for group work may become angry with the high achievement orientation of the others. The anger may result in conflict or it may result in withdrawal and apparent apathy. The members with higher achievement needs often perceive the members with lower achievement needs as unreliable and unlikely to work hard. They are thus tempted to do more of the work themselves to assure that their group makes at least a presentable showing. The members with lower achievement needs are then tempted to let the others go ahead and do the work if that is the way they feel about it. As the high achievers do more work the group becomes less and less rewarding to the others, and they contribute less and less. This reinforces the stereotype the workers have that they are burdened with a group composed of a few good, hard-working people and a number of drones, and so the cycle spirals and becomes vicious.

Members tend to vary also in their need for well-ordered work procedures. Some members will enjoy working in a task environment which is highly structured. They like to have agendas, deadlines, and carefully worked-out procedures which enable them to keep an eye on the time and to make productive use of their resources. They like to know what is expected of them and when. Other group members will find tightly organized work procedures stifling and prefer a more freewheeling and brainstorming approach. They will tend to want to leave the agenda when an exciting idea comes to them. They are not as concerned about reducing ambiguity and are not as worried about deadlines and the management of group time. Many members will fall somewhere between these two extremes and will like a working environment which has both some structure and some looseness. In groups containing people with a wide range of structure needs, the working out of suitable procedures for cooperative effort may bring those with needs for highly organized work environments into conflict with those who prefer less tightly structured procedures. Discovering and confronting these varying needs can often help members evolve procedures which are relatively freewheeling and unstructured as the group begins a new project and which later become more orderly as members come to a decision and start planning to achieve their goals. Although it is difficult to do, if groups can create a flexible work climate they can often become exceptionally productive. Such groups gain an added bonus from the creativity and novelty of the unstructured people during the opening phases of group problem-solving while retaining much of the structured members' administrative efficiency in the application phases when the group divides up work and mobilizes its resources.

An important part of the task conflicts of any work group will relate to the substance of the discussion. Groups may ignore such problems by simply ruling out certain topics from consideration. "We never talk about the honors program because Mary is in it and very excited about it and Joe tried it for a term and hated it." Members may smooth problems over and not raise the disagreements they feel, because of the anticipated unpleasant conflict. As a result, the group may well make poor decisions and some members may be less than committed to what the group is doing.

When a group brings task conflicts into the open they may decide rightly or wrongly that the conflict cannot be resolved. (Sometimes, indeed, conflicts are irreconcilable even in cooperative groups.) The group may then bring in a majority report and a minority report. Not all groups have the luxury of making two reports, however, and the external environment (for instance, the parent organization) may require one recommendation or decision. The majority may then submit its conclusions and the minority may have to accept them or withdraw. (Of course, sometimes high status members submit the conclusions and they are, in effect, a minority acting as a majority.) One might say that such a situation leaves the conflict unresolved and such procedures are unsatisfactory. Still, many conflict situations are handled in this manner and some at least are probably of such a nature that they cannot be worked through.

A group may bring a task conflict out into the open and discover great differences which they then resolve by negotiating a compromise. Usually the discussion quickly reveals two polar positions of considerable intensity within the group. One or more members, however, will be undecided (on the fence) or more committed to the group's coming to some decision than to either of the two polar positions. The middle-of-the-roaders will then try to work out some position which requires each of the conflicting camps to give a little in order to keep some of their important ideas in the final conclusion. If both sides are willing to give, and the negotiators in the middle are skillful, a compromise may be worked out that the members can support and work to achieve. Managing conflict by compromise is less than satisfactory for the members of the rival factions, and it may set a work norm which carries over to other tasks and other subjects, thus reducing group efficiency. Sometimes, however, compromises are wiser ways to manage conflict than majority or minority reports or splitting the group apart or resorting to violence.

A group may bring a task conflict out into the open and confront differences, come to some common ground positions, and work through to a consensus which all members can support wholeheartedly. During the conflict members may be stimulated to express all of their objections and disagreements forcibly and without reservation. The end result of confrontation and working through to consensus if often a thoroughly tested and wise decision or solution to which the members are committed. Such conflicts are productive in that they contribute to better problem-solving and wiser decisions.

Task conflicts about message content tend to relate to one or more of the following kinds of issues (1) questions of fact, (2) questions of policy, and (3) questions of value. Generally, groups find it easiest to work out conflicts relating to questions of fact. Questions of policy are difficult but consensus is often possible. Members who come into value conflict frequently cannot achieve satisfactory consensus.

Members of groups in task conflict should, therefore, sort out what kinds of issues divide them. If the issue is related to facts, they may be able to resolve the conflict by gathering additional information and by more careful testing of the available sources. If the group is studying whether or not there should be a change in the way instructors grade student work, they may come into conflict over the number of As, Bs, Cs, and Ds given in courses in psychology, sociology, and speech-communication as compared to the number given in chemistry, geology, physics, and mathematics. Conflicts over such matters are factual and the members can often resolve them by making further investigations and getting the distribution of grades by classes for the last several terms from the office of the registrar. Task groups which make decisions and try to solve problems on the basis of wrong information often fail to do a good job. All members, thus, have reason to try to agree on the basis of the best information available.

Closely related to the conflicts over factual matters are those differences that grow out of group problem-solving efforts. A group may face an important common problem, perhaps even a crisis situation, and seriously disagree about the nature and causes of their problem. Here again, careful investigation of the conditions surrounding their difficulty and thorough testing of possible reasons for the problem should aid the group in coming to consensus about their difficulty. Without productive resolution of conflict over the nature of the common problem, the members are likely to try solutions which leave them no better off than they were before. The feedback from other individuals, groups, and organizations to group messages resulting from collective problem-solving is often direct and clear and, when the attempts are unsuccessful, painful.

If the members come in conflict over questions of policy, the possibility of successful consensus is less than when the question can be convincingly resolved by observation of the facts. Questions of policy relate to the group's general philosophy and overall objectives as well as to the important courses of action they should follow. A policy question might be, What should the College of Liberal Arts do to improve grading procedures? Because policy questions often relate to matters of philosophy, they may arouse conflict relating to basic world view, ethical systems, and values of the members. Often members will come into conflict over the amount of resources, energy, or effort that the group should invest in various courses of action. The value questions, as we shall see, are the most difficult to resolve. However, if the group can find some common goal or common philosophical ground upon which they can all agree and which is broad enough to include the various courses of action under consideration, they often can work through their policy conflict to consensus. A very important step in such task-conflict resolution, therefore, is a careful consideration of where the members agree and where they disagree. If the group's attention can be focused first on areas of agreement and these commonalities can be kept in mind, then the conflict may be resolved by continually checking various positions against the common goals. Again, the task-oriented group provides a context in which such conflict resolution is facilitated because of the group's common task and purpose and the fact that success may generate additional value which all can share.

If the members come into conflict over questions of value, they will face many difficulties in trying to reach consensus. A value question might be, Ought one human being be given institutional authority to evaluate another publicly? One faction of a group may assert that it is ethically and morally deplorable for one person to have the right to evaluate another human being's intellectual effort and worth and to put down the evaluation in a public record which is available to the student's family, friends, enemies, and potential employers. Another faction may assert that evaluation is not only inevitable but necessary and therefore honest evaluation reflecting the actual worth of the student's work is not only desirable but the only ethically justifiable course for the faculty to follow. Polar positions on the basic question of the morality and value of grading itself reflect a conflict over values and are most difficult to resolve.

Many times groups will have to give up on the resolution of conflict over values and simply recognize that if they are to act as a unit they will have to work around or within the restrictions that the differing value systems place upon their efforts. Successful resolution of value conflicts usually requires *changing the value systems of some or all of the members.* People change their value systems reluctantly and usually only when the group has high saliency for them. That is, you are a member of a number of task-oriented small groups, and of other important groups, such as your family. Any given group can be compared to other groups as to how important it is in your life. You are not likely to change your value system in a classroom task-oriented small group that meets for five or six hours when your values are supported by another strong, salient group that has a long history.

Groups are a powerful technique for changing values as we saw in Part I in our discussion of the conversion style of small group communication. Conversion groups, however, meet for a period of weeks or months and are dedicated to the process of breaking up old value systems and building in new perspectives. Most task-oriented small groups cannot shift their attention to the conversion style for a period of months in order to change value systems. Of course, as task-groups continue to meet for long periods of time (for instance, if people work together in the same office for years), group pressures may gradually bring the value systems of the participants into more compatibility, but in the short run, changing values to resolve conflicts is an unlikely solution.

$$*$$

A Brief Review of Key Ideas in Part II

* The task-oriented small group is composed of three or more people working together to do a clearly specified job or to reach a common goal.

* Five is an excellent number for a work group.

* The first question in the mind of every person in a new work group is: How do I relate to these other people as a human being?

* Cohesiveness encourages productivity, morale, and communication.

* Role specialization in small work groups is inevitable. Role is a person's place in the group—the part he expects to play and that others expect him to play.

* A member's role is worked out jointly by the person and the group.

* Every new group must go through a "shakedown cruise" during which roles are tested. During this "shakedown cruise," secondary tensions mount.

* Although some roles are established quickly and easily, the role of leader is among the last to emerge. (Part III goes into this much more thoroughly.)

* Groups experience a dramatic increase in cohesiveness when their role structure becomes stable. They are then able to get on with their work more effectively.

* Groups develop norms or standard operating procedures dealing with both the task dimension and with social interactions.

* One of the most important features of group dynamics is the power of nonverbal and verbal communication to get people to act as others in the group do.

* As the group develops higher levels of cohesiveness, the pressure on group members to adopt the group's norms increases.

* Like individual habits, the group's norms can be changed.

* Unsatisfied needs are motivators of behavior.

* A little positive attention to the marginal individual, the potential "dead wood," will go a long way toward increasing cohesiveness.

* When primary or secondary tensions reach a certain level, the group finds it difficult to concentrate on its job. Tensions must be released, directly or indirectly.

* Agreement is one of the most basic social rewards.

* Disagreements are socially punishing but absolutely essential to good group work. A disagreement, to do its job, must be perceived as a disagreement.

* Good groups use the positive climate builders to knit the group back together after a decision is reached.

* Although much about the task-oriented small group is cooperative, it tends, in fact, to be a mixed-motive communication climate.

* Conflicts arise from the three major areas of social rewards: contention for leadership, task influence, and popularity.

* Groups often find conflicts in the social dimension difficult to deal with and take flight from them by ignoring them or smoothing them over.

* The best technique for the management of conflict in the social dimension of the task-oriented small group is to confront the problem and work it out.

* In working through the social conflicts, the members should focus on the group rather than scapegoating individuals.

* You cannot always tell from the content of the communication alone whether the conflict is a task disagreement or a problem in the social dimension.

*   The process of confronting task conflict and working through to a group consensus often results in a thoroughly tested and wise decision or solution to which all of the members are committed.

*   Groups often find conflict over questions of value the most difficult to resolve; conflict over policy somewhat easier to handle, and conflict over facts the least difficult to settle.

Check Your Grasp of the Dynamics of Good Groups

*(Complete all answers, then check
each answer on the pages given.)*

1. Define *cohesiveness.*

—page 48

2. Define *status* and relate it to *roles.*

—pages 51 and 52

3. List the ways in which a high status role can fulfill the needs of an individual.

—page 51, pages 64 and 65

4. Briefly describe the basic process that results in role specialization.

—pages 52 to 56

5. Briefly describe the way groups develop norms.

—pages 56 and 57

6. How may a group meet the needs on the deficit ladder?

—pages 62 to 66

7. List as many of the seven concrete steps to build cohesiveness as you can.

—pages 70 to 72

8. List the three positive social interactions discovered by Professor Bales.

—page 73

9. Why do people feel tense when they first start working in a new group?

—pages 73 and 74

10. How may a group learn to tolerate disagreements?

—pages 75 and 76

11. List and explain the three basic ways groups deal with conflict in the social dimension.

—pages 76 to 82

12. List and explain the three basic kinds of questions that cause conflict in the task dimension.

—pages 86 to 89

Part III   ✳ ✳ ✳ ✳

Objectives

After you have studied Part III you should be better able to:

* *observe the communication of members in newly formed groups and discover when the first phase of leadership contention is finished.*

* *note which members have been eliminated as leaders in the first phase.*

* *examine the contenders for leadership in the second phase, and if you are eliminated, select a good time to become a lieutenant for the best of those contending.*

* *if you are a contender in the second phase, read the verbal and nonverbal communication from the members to discover the type and style of leadership they want.*

* *respond quickly to situations, as they arise in a meeting, in a way that aids the group in reaching its common objective.*

* *exhibit role functions as an appointed leader or moderator that enable you to emerge as the natural, as well as the formal, leader of the group.*   .

* *have an approach planned to break the ice and get a meeting started.*

* *respond quickly to situations as they arise to assure the release of primary tension and create a positive social climate.*

* *respond quickly to situations as they arise to provide sufficient structure for the group to achieve its task objective.*

* *respond quickly to situations that generate secondary tension as they arise.*

Leadership

* *encourage the nonparticipant and draw the quiet person into the group.*

* *discourage the person who speaks too much and still keep the member as a productive participant.*

* *use Checklist 2, p. 158, as a basis for a thorough evaluation of a meeting.*

* *use Checklist 3, p. 159, as a basis for a thorough and clear-eyed evaluation of your own leadership in a meeting.*

PART III BUILDS UPON YOUR general understanding of group process and development, concentrating upon the role of leadership. Like so many of our everyday ideas about working with groups, leadership often means many different things to different people. Part III examines the various important meanings of leadership and concentrates on reporting results of study and research on the emergence of natural leaders and on the nature of formal leadership. This section deals with such questions as: How do natural leaders emerge in small task-oriented groups? What can I do to become the natural leader of my group? What is the relationship between being appointed a chairman or moderator (formal leadership) and being the natural leader of a group?

In addition, Part III answers some of the nagging little questions that plague any person who must lead a meeting, such as: How can I facilitate communication and save time with the use of questions? By the use of an agenda? What should I do to encourage participation? To discourage the person who dominates the meeting? What should I do to follow up the results of a meeting?

The Role of the Leader

We are of two minds. Of all the roles that emerge in a work group, none has fascinated philosophers, writers, social scientists, and the man on the street more than the top role, the top position. The high status, most influential role has been the subject of novels, dramas, poetry, conjecture, old wives' tales, folklore, and, of late, many scientific investigations.

When we talk of this role in common sense terms we usually refer to it as the *leadership role.* In our country we are of two minds about leadership. If a member of a test-tube group suggests that another person would be a good leader, the typical response is, "Oh, no! Not me. Someone else could do a better job." Despite such protests, nearly every member of the groups, when interviewed, said he or she would actually like to have been the leader, to have had his or her way, to have run things.

Why this ambivalence? On the one hand, our democratic traditions suggest that all people are created equal and that nobody is better than anybody else. We maintain a belief in a classless society. The candidate for office makes much of being an uncommon common man. He is just one of the folks, and he likes baseball, hunting, fishing, and hot dogs. The candidate does not even *seek* office. Only an egotist would publicly assert that he is better than other men and so deserves the job. Rather, he waits for a draft and when he is called, he humbly and modestly does his best to live up to "the high responsibility and great challenge." On the other hand, we love success. Top status positions are symbols of success. We work hard to get to the top. Young men, and increasingly with the rise of Women's Liberation young women, too, are expected to be successes and make something of themselves. They are educated for leadership, trained for leadership, and encouraged to become leaders.

The "now I want it, now I don't" feeling about leadership explains why we spend so much time investigating and studying leadership. Investigators have explained leadership by three major approaches: (1) the trait approach, (2) the styles of leadership approach, and (3) the contextual approach.

The trait approach. The earliest tradition of leadership assumes that leaders are born and not made. Leadership is inherent in the person, and one is destined to become a leader. In early times one was chosen of God or the gods; in more recent times an individual was thought to possess the proper leadership traits. In the early years of this century, social scientists explored the traits a person must have in order to become a leader. They measured all sorts of characteristics to see if they were related to leadership. They measured the weight and height of leaders and nonleaders. They gave vocabulary, intelligence, and personality tests to many people. In 1948, Professor R. M. Stogdill, a psychologist, published a study entitled "Personal Factors Associated with Leadership: A Survey of the Literature." He was unable to find in the literature any pattern of inherent personality traits that would explain leadership. The notion that leaders are born and not made just did not stand up under careful and systematic study.

The styles of leadership approach. Next, the students of leadership investigated the question of whether or not they could find an ideal style of leadership. Much of the work was done in organizational settings, particularly in business and industry. Researchers examined authoritarian, democratic, and *laissez-faire* (hands-off) styles of leadership. They compared autocratic with democratic, group-centered with leader-centered, production-oriented with employee-oriented leadership and management. One school of industrial psychologists and management experts developed an approach to *participative* management, which was essentially democratic management. The first results seemed to indicate clear superiority in terms of morale and productivity for the democratic style of leadership. Nevertheless, as more research accumulated, some groups were found to do well with a more directive or authoritarian style. The surgeon in the operating room was authoritarian; so was the football coach. Clearly, the purpose of the group and the kind of work it had to do played a part in determining the best "style" of leadership for that particular group.

The contextual approach. The most satisfactory explanation of leadership is furnished by the approach that says leadership is a result of the individual traits (inherited characteristics plus training), the purposes of the group, the pressures put on the group from the outside, and the way the persons in the group talk, work, and relate with one another. This view recognizes that some people learn to play the game of "being leader" and that they tend to have certain opening moves that they use in starting the game whenever they join a new work group. To some extent, the way they try to be leader depends upon what they think about the group. They do not approach the squad at basic training in the Army with the same expectations that they do a peer discussion group. The sergeant tends to be "bossy," while the moderator of the discussion group tends to be democratic. Our approach is the contextual view, and the test-tube groups explain the way a *leader* emerges during the course of a group working on a job. Such an explanation provides a more complete view of leadership than either the trait approach or the one-best-style approach. It includes the idea that leaders are to some extent "born," but it also suggests that potential leaders can achieve skills and improve talents. The contextual approach, the consideration of the total context, or all components, of each instance of "a group," explains why a person who emerges as leader in one group may fail to emerge as the leader of a second, apparently similar, group. It also accounts for successful groups that follow leaders who have quite different styles of leadership.

The Way Leaders Emerge

The descriptive model of leadership emergence. If we dip a glass of water in the ocean and then allow it to stand until the water evaporates, the salt that is left is a *residue.* If we try to pick out the salt before the water evaporates, we have quite a job. In like fashion the group does not pick a leader. Rather, it eliminates people from consideration until one person is left. The test-tube groups select their leaders *by the method of residues.*

The one outstanding feature of the reports people make of the early meetings of a work group is that while they cannot say who will emerge as the leader, they have little difficulty agreeing on who will *not* be the leader. People look first for clues that will eliminate others from high status roles. Ruling people out helps them concentrate their attention on the remaining contenders. Moreover, when someone picks another as a potential leader, he has to shut the door on his own hopes. People like to leave that door open.

The descriptive emergence model of group process, thus, explains leadership emergence as well as the development of other roles. The general pattern of the way leaders emerge consists of two phases. The first is relatively short. During this time, the group eliminates people who are clearly unsuitable. The second is much longer, and during this phase, the remaining serious contenders battle it out for support.

The first phase. In case studies at the University of Minnesota, roughly one-half of the participants were ruled out in the first phase. First to go were those who "did not take part." Next, the group eliminated those who, though active, seemed uninformed, ignorant, or unskilled at the task. It was felt these members did not know much, or that they "didn't make much sense." And finally, some very active and vociferous participants were eliminated because they took strong, unequivocal stands. They expressed their position in flat, unqualified assertions, and impressed upon the others that they would not change their minds no matter what. They were perceived as being "too extreme" or "too inflexible."

Phase two. The second part of the process was characterized by intensified competition among the remaining members. Members felt irritated and frustrated. The group was wasting time and "nothing was accomplished." This was the toughest part of the "shakedown cruise." Animosities developed among some of the participants. The group began to run away from the question of leadership. Sometimes they found scapegoats to account for their failures. Secondary tensions rose to uncomfortable levels. Conflict often developed.

To illustrate the way groups select leaders, we will outline two typical and successful paths that many groups used to steer a course through the second phase.

(1) *Path one.* The first is a relatively short and easy way through the struggle for leadership. We will use the basic group composed of Joe, Harry, Bill, Don, and Wilbur. Let us say that Joe is eliminated because he is quiet, and Don is eliminated because he seems uninformed. Wilbur has assumed the role of tension releaser and is thus eliminated as a potential leader. This concludes the first phase. Bill and Harry remain in contention. During the second phase, as both try to give orders and divide up work, Joe decides that Harry is capable but arbitrary and tactless. He finds Bill capable, sensible, and understanding. Joe begins to support Bill whenever Bill makes a leadership move. He voices his support. He *agrees* and says, "That's a good idea. Let's do it that way." At this point, Joe emerges in the role of *lieutenant.* The emergence of a lieutenant is a key development in deter-

mining leadership. Bill, if he gains a strong lieutenant, is in a much better position to emerge as a leader.

After another period of contention, Wilbur begins to side with Bill and Joe. In short order, Don swings over and Bill has emerged as leader. When this happens the group will experience a considerable release of social tension and a corresponding increase in cohesiveness. Not all of their role problems have been solved, however. Harry is a potential source of trouble. He may be upset enough to try to sabotage the group. He is one of the more capable members or he would not have remained in contention in the second phase. When he loses his bid for leadership he is frustrated and upset. He usually finds Bill personally obnoxious and is irritated with Joe for supporting Bill's ideas. Bill and Harry typically are in the midst of a personality conflict.

Good groups knit people like Harry back into the group in a productive, useful, and high status role such as a task expert or an information-source person. Many groups failed at this crucial point. The newly emerged leader often has considerable animosity for the loser. Bill will typically find Harry unreasonable and troublesome. He thinks of Harry as a potential source of trouble. The greatest mistake that he can make at this point is to give in to the human tendency to exploit the power of his new role as leader to make life miserable for Harry. If Bill does "rub Harry's nose in it," he can expect trouble as long as Harry remains in the group. Bill should remember that *the newly emerged leader is always on probation. If he does not work out, he will be deposed.* Some of the new leaders who punished their opponents lost their positions because of this. The others decided that if that was the way the leader dealt with the opposition, they did not want him for their leader. The wise leader, with support from his lieutenant and the others, always took pains at this crucial point to support the loser and to encourage him in another productive role.

(2) *Path two.* The second way of finding a leader is more frustrating and difficult than the first. We will return to our basic group at the point where Bill gained a lieutenant, Joe. Had the group taken path two, at this point Wilbur would

have found Harry's style of leading more to his liking than Bill's. Perhaps Wilbur has a greater appreciation for Harry's wry humor, and he finds that Harry's skill in thinking through problems more than compensates for his bluntness. Wilbur thus becomes Harry's *lieutenant.* Now the group works two against two with Don becoming the "swing vote." Such groups may continue the second phase for a long time before Don casts a consistent deciding vote. In one of the case studies at Minnesota, the group continued for several weeks deadlocked in this fashion until one of the contenders turned to the swing vote and asked him directly, "Where do you stand?" The member replied, "Right in the middle." Of course, the struggle continued.

If the problems become too frustrating, the members may decide that they lack leadership; so they hold an election. If the group is not ready to really follow either Harry or Bill, they will take flight from the leadership struggle by electing someone who was eliminated in the first phase — perhaps a quiet woman, or in the case of our prototype group, they would probably elect Don because he is neutral. People in Don's position, when elected leader, will usually accept the job and *begin acting like a leader.* No matter how quiet and uninvolved their manner has been up to that point, they change drastically and begin to take charge. The others do not follow, however, and within a short period of time, Don will cease to act like a leader, and Bill and Harry will continue the contention until Don swings his support to Bill. Wilbur's move at this juncture is crucial. Should he stay committed to Harry, the group may be doomed to work without clear leadership or stable roles. However, Wilbur has demonstrated a preoccupation with social matters, and he is alert to the secondary tensions. Since he is a buddy of Harry's, he is in an excellent position to swing his support to Bill, joke away the tensions, and conciliate Harry into a productive role.

The Lessons of Leadership Emergence

The yardstick for leadership is the group's goal. The members spend time and energy on leadership because it is so important to the success of the group. We are very touchy about the people who "boss" us around. We do not like to take orders. If we have to, we prefer a leader who gives wise orders in a way we can tolerate. The leader will make crucial suggestions and decisions about the way the work will be divided and the way the material resources of the group will be distributed. In the end, the group rejects potential leaders until they are left with the person who seems best able to lead *for the good of all.*

In some groups leaders fail to emerge. Sometimes the struggle for leadership is never resolved. Such groups become invalids. The members spend their time in backbiting and getting back at internal enemies. If after the first phase a group is left with two or three potential leaders, each having substantial handicaps, the leadership may not be resolved. For example, one group was left with two persons in contention. One had a strong, agressive style of organizing the work. She took charge and "came on strong." She was perceived as being too dictatorial and bossy. The other was much more congenial and less aggressive. She had more understanding of the esteem and social needs of the group. However, the group soon discovered that, though she had definite human relations skills, her thinking was fuzzy and tentative. She also proved to be indecisive. The first individual was clearly the more capable of the two in developing coherent courses of action, but . . . On balance, the two contenders were equally handicapped. As a result, the group was unwilling to follow either.

Central persons. Some people have developed opening moves as they search for a role in a new work group that fascinate the others. They may be positive or negative people; we shall call them *central* persons. A central person may be a "star." She may be unusually capable and a potential asset to the group's productivity, or she may be exceptionally skillful at human relations, unusually charming. A central person who would be a great threat to the group would be a member who seems extremely hostile to the group and its purposes or someone who downgrades the work. She may make it plain she feels the others in the group are incapable. At any rate, her attitude becomes a central concern to the group. Sometimes a central person is someone who is unusually apathetic and uninvolved, who simply refuses to take part in the group. All of these people tend to take the group's attention away from its tasks.

A common threatening central person is the *manipulator.* He comes to the group with the intention of exploiting it for his own ends. He intends to take it over and run it. Manipulators tend to be either *hard sell* or *soft sell.* The hard-sell manipulator usually comes on strong. He talks a great deal and takes charge immediately with a strong hand. "Let's get down to business. Now here's what we will do." When the group resists his leadership, he tries to argue and browbeat the others into line. When someone challenges him, the others will swing to support the contender. Often the hard-sell manipulator then stands alone against the group, trying hard to talk everyone down. On other occasions, the hard-sell manipulator finds no one who will challenge him immediately. He then is certain that he has succeeded in taking over. When he gives orders, however, they are not followed. People continually misunderstand, or they fail to follow through. He decides that he has not been "working hard enough" at his leading, so he begins to give his orders slowly, carefully, in simple English as though he were talking to morons. This arouses even greater resentment and "goldbricking." He decides that they are all lazy and irresponsible. Inevitably, another contender emerges and becomes leader. The manipulator is now extremely frustrated. His self-image is badly dented. He came into the group confident of his superiority and his ability to run the group "his way," and the group has rejected him. He seldom examines where he has failed. Usually he turns on the group; they are ignorant and stupid. If he remains in the group, he is often a troublemaker. Finding him an acceptable role takes ingenuity.

The soft-sell manipulator is often much more successful in his second phase. He often emerges for a time as the leader. He has many "tricks" and "formulas" of human relations at his command. He is friendly and congenial. He seems less bossy and more democratic. He sizes up the group to see whom he can "con" and who will be troublesome for him. He does more work outside the group's formal meetings, like chatting with this or that member over coffee. He is a "politician." After several weeks of working together, however, the others find him out. They discover that he is getting his way and that under his apparently congenial and democratic facade, he is using the group for his personal ends. When the soft-sell manipulator is found out, a challenger comes forward, and the group must reshuffle roles until a new leader emerges.

Effect of changing personnel. In some test-tube groups a new member was deliberately introduced after a leader had emerged and the roles stabilized. In others, a member was removed, and in still others, a member was removed and a new person inserted in her place. In all instances, a change in personnel proved unsettling. If a new person was added, this person brought with her a complement of skills and talents, and a role had to be found for her. All of the roles had to be reshuffled to free enough of the duties to form a slot for the new individual. When a member was removed, a role struggle also resulted. Her tasks had to be assumed by the remaining members. If she had important duties, the members who stood to gain by *climbing* upward on the status ladder came into conflict. Likewise, when a member was replaced, the new person did not take over the same role that the former member had; more reshuffling of all roles was necessary.

The effect of changing personnel by adding, removing, or replacing individuals is a repeat of the "shakedown cruise." The typical result is a period of role instability and struggle that surprises and frustrates the members. People often do not understand what is going on and why it must go on. They respond by blaming the new member. "Everything was fine until he came." Or they bemoan the loss of a member. "Before Joan left, everything went along fine; we sure miss Joan."

Effect of appointing a leader. What happens to the test-tube groups when one of the members is appointed the leader? This is an extremely important question because so many work groups have an appointed supervisor, foreman, chief, manager, head, chairperson, or boss. Appointing a leader had three interesting effects on, but did not change, the *fundamental* pattern of leader emergence.

(1) *Appointed leader takes over.* The appointed leader immediately *began to act like a leader.* At first the group looked to the appointed leader for leadership. However, after he had led for a time and they had followed in a tentative way, his leadership was challenged by one or two of the other members. The challenge came at the end of the first phase of the leadership struggle. This was a turning point for the appointed leader. If he acted hurt and thought that because he was appointed leader they ought to follow him, he was well on his way to being rejected.

(2) *The role struggle facilitated.* When after a brief challenge the appointed leader demonstrated he was a good choice for the job, the members quickly followed his lead and the second phase of the leadership struggle was short and easy. If the appointed leader was the person who would have emerged as natural leader of the group, assigning him the job made the "shakedown cruise" much smoother.

(3) *The role struggle prolonged.* The third effect of assigning a leader was to slow down the process of having a natural leader emerge. In such a case, the assigned leader took charge, was followed, challenged, and then deposed, and a new leadership struggle began. The "shakedown cruise" was long and rough for these groups. The assigned leader had lost his position and esteem. The group had to find a productive role for him or be plagued with a disgruntled member in a formal position of leadership.

Seven Concrete Steps to Natural Leadership

From the Minnesota studies of test-tube groups we have developed a profile of the talk and action that often resulted in a member emerging as leader. You should understand that even if you talk and act this way in a given group, it is no guarantee that you will become the natural leader. Another member may do and say these things in a way the others in the group find more to their liking. However, people who do not understand groups quite seldom do or say very many of these things at all. Here, conscious competence leads to success because so few people realize how natural leaders emerge in work groups.

Do not be a manipulator. The most certain way to assure being eliminated as a leader is to act and talk in such a way that the others perceive that you are attempting to manipulate them or the group. We all belong to groups in which we have a sincere interest. We are dedicated to their welfare and feel no desire to manipulate them. A good salesman knows that he must be sold on his product to sell it to others. The member who emerges as the natural leader must be sincerely and completely dedicated to the welfare of the group.

Be willing to pay the price. To emerge as the natural leader you must want to help the group enough to do the work. Almost everyone would like the rewards of leadership, but not every member is willing to work "above and beyond the call of duty" for the good of all. People who emerge as leaders make personal sacrifices for the group. They work overtime, inconvenience themselves, and tackle even low status tasks with enthusiasm. Members who emerge as leaders are willing to arouse resentment and take criticism. The group requires that its leader make some of the tough decisions. Harry Truman said of the presidency, "The buck stops here." Certainly this is true of work groups. When painful decisions about distributing rewards unequally, for example, must be made, the group usually pushes them on the leader. Such decisions inevitably arouse resentment. The person who emerges as leader must demonstrate that she is tough enough to make such decisions wisely and take the criticism.

Talk up. If you wish to be leader, you must take an active interest in the group's work. You must make a contribution. Your talk and action must show an active commitment to the group, a concern and consideration for the others as people, and an understanding of the task. Remember, however, that the person who talks a lot but who seems to be a manipulator, or who seems inflexible, or uninformed, does not emerge as leader.

Do your homework. If you wish to be a leader, you must know what is going on. Members who emerge as leaders have sensible ideas and state them clearly. They know things that will help the group. Be informed about the group's work. Plan for the good of the group. Put in extra time working out ways to improve the group and to help it achieve its goals. Members who emerge as leaders demonstrate that they can provide workable and efficient plans of action.

Make personal sacrifices. Nothing tells the others more clearly that you are sincere and not a manipulator than your willingness to make personal sacrifices for the group. The manipulator gets his way at the expense of the group. The natural leader gets the group's way at his or her personal expense. Volunteering to aid the group or to help members work for the group is evidence of your sincerity. Members who emerge as leaders do not worry about who gets credit for work or for ideas. They often give credit offered to them to others. People who worry about recognition that *their* plan, or *their* way, or *their* ideas are used seldom emerge as leaders.

Raise the status of other members. Closely related to the fact that leaders do not worry about getting credit for their work is their tendency to raise the status of other members. They compliment other people when they do something for the group. They indicate that every person in the group is significant and is making a contribution. They seek out ways to make other people feel important. In short, you are more likely to emerge as an esteemed leader if you forget about it and work as hard as you can to make the group a good one.

Build group cohesiveness. In Part II we suggested seven steps (pages 70-72) to build cohesiveness. Members who emerge as leaders do many of these things. They communicate their interest in the group and its welfare. They help build a history and a tradition.

Formal Leadership

Test-tube groups and real-life groups. Most of our groups are not composed of peers and everyone does not start out equal. Most work groups function within a *formal* organization. The salesperson works *under* a sales manager within a corporation. Student governments have presidents and their committees have chairpersons. The executive committee of the PTA chapter functions within the larger organization. People come to such work groups with different status. Sometimes the status is internal to the organization, such as the dean meeting with a group of students. Sometimes the status is external to the group, such as having a famous surgeon and a famous financier meeting on the same committee for the campus development fund. Although such status differences introduce complications, the basic process of group development can be adjusted to take these into account. In other words, test-tube groups do tell us about real-life meetings, about real-life groups. We haven't the space to make applications to all the many variations of work groups, but we will show the way leadership emergence is related to the management of organizational work groups. With this application as a guide you can make similar modifications of the principles to fit other situations.

Formal position. Organizations usually have a formal structure. Members simply do not have enough contact with all other people in a large organization to form impressions about them. Certainly they do not work together enough to develop a role structure. *Formal positions* take the place of roles and tell a given person what the organization expects from him and what he can expect from the organization. The formal positions may be blueprinted into a table of organization:

Figure 3 is part of a typical table of organization. The duties of each position may be written out so that each person who fills that position knows what he or she must do *and* what he must not do. The status relationships are spelled out as well. The bigger the box and the closer to the top, the higher the status of the position. Each position has certain tasks associated with it. No matter who fills box A, that person is expected to hire and fire the people in boxes B, C, D, and E. He or she may have the duty of making and implementing plans. The position will also carry the right to reward or punish those in positions below. The duties can be thought of as *responsibilities.* If the duties are not taken care of, the organization will call the person in the position to account. Associated with the duties and sanctions of each position is a certain amount of *authority*. The authority goes with the position and is inherited by every person who takes it over. A certain amount of *prestige* also goes along with each position. This prestige adheres to every individual who fills the formal position.

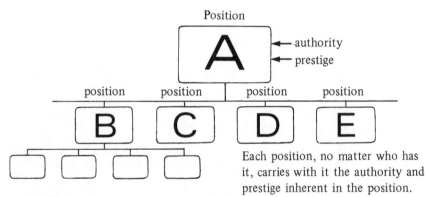

Each position, no matter who has it, carries with it the authority and prestige inherent in the position.

Figure 3

By placing people in the table of organization, we add new dimensions to the properties inherent in the positions themselves. Power is added to the authority in a certain position, and esteem to the prestige. Power is the effective exercise of authority and is, thus, a function of the authority inherent in the position plus the role that the person develops in the work groups to which he or she belongs.

A certain amount of prestige adheres to every person who fills the particular position. However, when one assumes a position, one begins to work out a role in the informal work groups. In that process a person earns a certain amount of *esteem*. Esteem is not

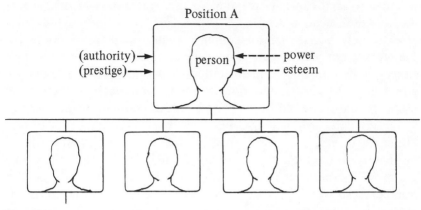

Figure 4

inherent in the position; it must be earned. *Thus power and esteem are both parts of the role that a person comes to play in the actual groups* that do the organization's work.

Formal leadership and natural leadership. The formal structure of an organization is static. It is set. The informal work groups that develop and change with a turnover in personnel and with fluctuating working conditions are dynamic. They constantly change, a little, or a lot. Frequently the informal organization, that is, the power and esteem that members earn, departs from the formal organization. The map no longer fits the realities. You cannot tell about a person's power and esteem by finding out his or her place in the formal table of organization. When formal leadership departs from natural leadership, trouble often follows. The real "boss" may not be the person with the title. What then?

The role struggle between a person with the formal position to help him in his battle for control and an individual with the esteem and power furnished by his standing with the members can be long and bloody. One example will show how group process applies to the problems of formal leadership. Let's say that a person in a position of formal leadership leaves the organization, and let's assume that the replacement is a stranger to the members in the work group. The entire role structure of that group will undergo a "shakedown cruise"! We use the example of a male manager here because the pattern of response to frustration we describe has been often observed in males. Of course, women assuming management positions face the same period of testing. We do not, as yet, know whether women typically respond to the frustrations of the "shake-down cruise" as do males.

The new manager must assume certain leadership functions for the work group because the formal position says that he must. He is expected by top management and by the organization to lead his group immediately. He will not, however, be accepted as the natural leader of the group without a period of testing. He must find his role in the informal groups within his department according to the basic principles of group process. When he finally assumes his role, it will be slightly different from that of the former manager, and the whole group will experience a reshuffling of roles. He does have certain standard levers furnished by the organization to help him emerge as leader. These may include the power to increase salaries, give bonuses, promote workers, and assign jobs and vacations and the right to punish tardiness, malingering, and poor work. You may think that these levers give the new manager an insurmountable advantage. Wisely used by a person who understands the dynamics of small groups, they may. Sometimes, however, the authority to punish and reward members turns out to be a handicap rather than a help.

Here is how it might happen. The new manager, whoever he is, is a marked man! His boss is watching closely to see how he will work out. He tries to do an exceptionally good job. The members of the group watch him even more carefully. Will he turn out to be a man they can follow? If he begins with strong and decisive leadership moves, he can expect some resistance. He may also find that he is misunderstood. Misunderstanding directions is a common way of resisting an order. To a man on trial, eager to prove his efficiency, such response may lead to frustration and anger. The new manager has now come to a crucial point. If he controls his anger and asks, "What have I done wrong . . . ?" he may be able to go back and mend his fences and start to build a role of leadership within the group. If he understands the way people emerge as natural leaders, he may win the power and esteem that the authority and prestige of his. job deserve and without which he must remain ineffective and unsatisfied to some extent. If he lashes back and pulls the levers by which he can force members to obey, he will start a spiral effect that results in malingering, more crises, less work, and trouble with his superiors. If he panics and decides that the trouble with his group is that he has not been firm enough, he may wildly put pressure on his people. He will lay down the law, read off the lazy workers, make sure that his directions are crystal clear, and supervise the most minute details of the work.

The members of his unit will then reject him as their leader, and someone else will emerge as the natural leader—the one to whom they all go with their gripes. Any new manager who starts down this toboggan ride will soon reach a point where more of his time and energy will be devoted to internal crises and struggling with members of his group than to his work. Such groups disturb their members. The morale declines. Members have difficulty talking about anything but their troubles. They vent their spleen on "him" and on any members who have sold out to "him." They plot and plan ways to get back at "him."

Although our example applied the knowledge about the small group to a hypothetical business organization, the same principles apply to the newly elected president of a fraternity or sorority, the chairperson of a college department, or the chairperson of an urban action group.

Techniques for Leading the Meeting

Directing the meeting. Research indicates two situations in which people will willingly accept direction from the conference leader. The first is when he is the natural leader of the group. The second is when a group of relative strangers are meeting only once. Assuming a willingness to follow his direction, the leader will still need certain basic skills in order to conduct an efficient meeting. The three basic techniques for this purpose are: the question, the summary, and the directive. Summaries are always useful to indicate progress and to orient the group. The democratic style requires a higher proportion of questions to directives; the authoritarian style, more directives than questions.

(1) *Getting the meeting started.* The first problem is to get the group down to business. A certain amount of time should be devoted to releasing primary tension, but then the group must go to work. Questions are very useful. Open-ended questions are asked in such a way that they cannot be answered with a simple "yes" or "no." An open-ended question can get things started. The leader should set the

mood for short and to-the-point comments early. If the first comment runs too long, the leader may have to interrupt with a question directed to someone else.

(2) *Keeping to the point.* An agenda, wisely used, will increase the efficiency of a meeting. The agenda should not be too long. Too often, we are overly optimistic about what can be accomplished in a meeting of an hour or an hour and a half. (It is unwise to run meetings much longer than two hours.) Keeping the agenda short assures adequate time for real communication. Do not expect the group to march through the steps of the agenda like a computer. Individuals, when they are thinking hard, do not organize their thoughts in outline fashion, and groups must kick an idea around a little, too. Decisions emerge from work sessions much as roles emerge. Too often we judge a meeting inefficient because the discussion wandered from the agenda. Sometimes the bypath is unnecessary and a waste of time, but some jumping from topic to topic is absolutely essential. This is the way decisions emerge in the work group.

The leader needs to watch carefully, therefore, and make running choices about the drift of the discussion. Is it part of the necessary "kicking around of an idea?" Is it a waste of time? He should not take the easy way out and make the choice on the letter of the agenda. When he decides that it is a waste of time, he should bring the meeting back to the agenda. Questions are most useful for this: "Can we tie this in with the point about the language requirement?" "Just a minute; how does this relate to the liberal arts?" Summaries can give an overview of the last few minutes of the meeting and leave the group on the agenda. Finally, a leader may simply assert that they are off the track and direct that they get back. "We seem to be getting off the subject. Let's get back to Bill's point."

(3) *Moving the meeting along.* We have emphasized the importance of not pushing the group too fast. Now we remind the leader that devoting twenty minutes to material that is worth five will cause restlessness and frustration. The leader should watch for signs that a topic has been exhausted. If members begin to repeat themselves, fidget, or pause for lack of

something to say, the leader should move to the next item. The summary is the best way to do so. A summary rounds off the discussion of a point and leads naturally to a new one. It also gives the group a feeling of accomplishment.

(4) *Coming to a decision.* From time to time the group will need to make decisions. The leader can help if he steps in at those points and asks, "Are we in substantial agreement on this point?" If the question is important he may call for a vote.

Applying group process to difficult situations. Often some tension-producing behavior creates an awkward moment for the leader and the participants. If the awkward situation is related to a role struggle within a work group, or if it is a result of inept communication skills on the part of the members, the insights from Part I and Part II should be used to work a permanent cure. Bringing the problem out into the open and discussing it is a good way. What we offer here are hints as to how to handle awkward situations immediately when they crop up in a given meeting — the "aspirin" of group treatment.

IF A GROUP MEMBER CREATES A PROBLEM

Symptoms	Reasons	What to do
Member won't participate.	Excessive primary tension. Feels lack of acceptance and status.	Involve him in conversation. Find out about his personal interests. Listen with interest to what he says. Devote some time to him, outside the discussion. When he does take part, make a special note of it. "That is a good point, Joe. We haven't been hearing enough from you. We appreciate hearing your position." Use questions to draw him out. Ask a direct, open-ended question so that only he can answer. Do not use a question than can be answered "yes" or "no," and, of course, do not ask a question that he might be unable to answer for lack of information.

Symptoms	Reasons	What to do
Member is joker, life of the party.	Feels tension, wants to relieve it. Enjoys spotlight and likes to get laughs.	Encourage him when tensions need release. Laugh, compliment his wit. Ignore him when it is time to go to work and tensions are eased. He will soon learn that his role is the productive release of tensions and that he mustn't waste time laughing it up when the group should be discussing.
Member monopolizes discussion.	(a) Is involved in a role struggle. Is trying to impress group to achieve high status or leadership.	(a) Encourage her if she is contending for role that will benefit the group the most. If not, interrupt her and move to another discussant. In general, encourage the group to take care of her.
	OR	
	(b) Is full of the subject and is sincerely eager to get to work.	(b) Don't embarrass him or be sarcastic. You will need him in this role later. Do not let him monopolize or give long speeches. Interrupt politely and throw the ball to another discussant with a question.
Member is argumentative, obstinate.	(a) Involved in role struggle.	(a) Keep your own temper. Understand she is not inherently obstinate but is so in the context of this discussion. Don't let the group get too tense and excited. Antagonism breeds further antagonism and secondary tension. Remember, group is partly responsible for her behavior. What can group do to change it?
	OR	

Symptoms	Reasons	What to do
	(b) Has strong personal convictions on topic.	(b) Examine his position carefully. Find merit in it if possible. Do not close your mind to the ideas just because they are expressed in an opinionated way. The group must examine all sides. In an emergency tell him time is short and you will be glad to talk to him later. Talk to him privately before the next meeting. Explain that his view is important, the group will consider it, but he must not destroy group effectiveness.

IF THE GROUP CREATES A PROBLEM

Symptoms	Reasons	What to do
Group is tired, apathetic, dull.	Marked lack of interest, low response rate, tired, yawning, quiet, polite.	Primary tension.	Small talk, joshing, kidding, humor. Make them smile, chuckle, laugh. Display as much enthusiasm and energy as you can. Do not give up if the first attempts to release the tension fail — keep pumping enthusiasm until it is caught. Explain subject vividly, ask lots of easy questions, play the devil's advocate.
Group is resistant, antagonistic, hostile.	Members intent on showing off, justifying their ideas, proving their worth. Members argue, come in conflict, show personal antagonism.	Secondary tensions caused by role and status struggles.	Analyze member ability. Assess the most useful role for each. Agree and support members who assume suitable roles. When secondary tensions become distracting, joke, use humor (not ridicule or satire), change the subject. Remind the group of its objectives. If necessary, face situation and bring role struggles into the open — talk about the social interactions.

Symptoms	Reasons		What to do
Group is enthusiastic, responsive, active.	Members stimulate one another to ideas, enthusiastic agreement. Everyone interested and involved.	Stable role structure. High level of feedback. Members forget themselves in their interest in topic.	Give the group its head. Do not worry too much about sticking to the planned agenda. The chaff can be sifted out later. Right now exploit the group's creativity.
Group is lost, confused, wants to go to work.	Members ask directions. Complain that they have been wasting time. Feel that the discussion lacks organization. Members say they want to do something.	Group has found its role structure. Wants to leave social matters and get down to work.	Now is time to suggest a way of working. Provide division of work, provide agendas and suggestions for systematic ways to go about discussion. (If you do this in "shakedown cruise" it will be rejected or resisted. If you provide structure now it will be welcomed.)

*

A Brief Review of Key Ideas in Part III

* The group does not pick a leader; rather, it eliminates people from consideration until one person emerges as leader.

* The second phase of the leadership struggle is the toughest part of the "shakedown cruise."

* The emergence of a lieutenant is a key development in determining leadership.

* The newly emerged leader is always on probation. If she does not work out, she will be deposed.

* If a group is forced to elect a leader before they are ready to make this decision, they will take flight by electing a clearly unsuitable leader.

* If a clearly unsuitable leader is appointed or elected, he will begin to act like a leader, but no one will follow him.

* A leader who best serves the needs of the entire group will emerge from the group.

* One of the most negative persons is a manipulator who comes to the group with the intention of exploiting it for his own ends.

* When a group changes personnel, a period of role instability and struggle will follow.

* If an appointed leader is satisfactory, she will emerge as the natural leader after a brief and easy testing time.

* If an appointed leader is unsatisfactory, she will be deposed and a new natural leader will emerge after a long and difficult testing time.

* Leaders cannot be imposed on the group. The leader must earn the right to lead even if he has been appointed a *formal* leader.

* Authority and prestige are associated with a formal position.

* Power and esteem are associated with the person's role in her group as well as with her formal position in the organization.

* The formal structure is static; the informal working relationships (the roles) are dynamic.

* When formal leadership departs from natural leadership, trouble often follows.

Check Your Grasp of Leadership

*(Complete all answers, then check
each answer on the pages given.)*

1. Compare the trait approach with the contextual approach to leadership.

—pages 100 to 102

2. List the reasons why some members are quickly eliminated as potential leaders.

—pages 102 and 103

3. Discuss the role of the *lieutenant* in the second phase.

—pages 103 and 104

4. Why is the role of the leader often the last one to emerge?

—pages 105 and 106

5. Define *central person*.

—page 106

6. Why does the manipulator fail in his bid for leadership?

—page 107

7. What is the effect of assigning a committee chairperson on the emergence of natural leadership?

—pages 108 and 109

8. List as many of the steps to emerging as a leader as you can remember. (There are seven.)

—pages 108 to 111

9. Compare and contrast the authority of an organizational position with the power of the man who fills that position.

—pages 111 to 113

10. Compare and contrast the prestige of an organizational position with the esteem of the person who fills that position.

—pages 111 to 113

IV

Part IV   ✳✳✳✳

Objectives

After you have studied Part IV you should be better able to:

*   *estimate how much work a group can do in a given period of time.*

*   *understand the process of decision emergence.*

*   *make a sound evaluation of a group meeting in terms of its task efficiency based upon a realistic expectation of how groups work.*

*   *tolerate the sometimes disruptive and aimless flight-taking of groups hard at work.*

*   *analyze the informal groups and communication channels in an organization.*

*   *anticipate the response of a losing group in a competitive situation and help the group become more effective.*

*   *anticipate the response of a winning group in competition and help the group continue its winning ways.*

*   *recognize the nature of groups in other than organizational contexts and help in planning and participating in such sessions.*

*   *recognize the causes of group competition and conflict within an organization.*

The Task Dimension of Groups

THE TASK DIMENSION OF GROUP PROCESS is as important to successful group effort as is the social dimension, although "personality conflicts" are often more dramatic and exciting than disagreements relating to the processing of information. Perhaps for that reason early studies of group dynamics tended to emphasize questions of leadership, group cohesiveness, norms, personality traits, interpersonal liking and conflict. Recent investigations, however, have examined the way good groups actually make decisions and solve problems. We now have a relatively detailed and accurate picture of group work. The research indicates that the conventional wisdom contains an unrealistic picture of good group work. The result is that many people evaluate meetings against an unrealistic standard of success and thus find group work frustrating.

Part IV describes the unrealistic picture of group work which is a part of much of the conventional wisdom and contrasts it with a realistic description of group process as revealed by the research. The section considers such topics as the basic emergent model of decision-making, the way to plan and participate in the task-dimension of group process, the influence of the organizational context upon group decision-making, intergroup conflict and communication, and cooperative and competitive group communication. The section concludes with a survey of the task communication of groups in other contexts such as negotiations, brainstorming sessions, and public discussion groups.

An Unrealistic Picture of Group Work

In the first three parts of this book we described the complexities of the social structuring, the norm development, and the role emergence in a small group. In this part we will examine the equally complex nature of the way groups work on a task. We cannot stress too strongly that working together in a group is a most difficult and complicated communication task. Given the fact that a small group meeting is such a complicated business, why is it that so many people think that it is a simple matter?

Many people prefer a simple view of groups because to recognize the difficulty of working productively in group meetings is to admit that they, as individuals, may be inadequate communicators. Many business and professional leaders spend years of study and work to become experts in some technical field such as engineering, medicine, certified public accounting, marketing research, income tax law, or security analysis. When they find themselves in managerial positions because of their outstanding success in a technical field, they discover that they spend more and more time communicating and less and less time practicing their specialities. They go to a continual round of conferences and meetings. If they admit the importance and complexity of communication, they must also admit that, despite their technical competence, they are unskilled in an important area of management. Such an admission is a confession of incompetency. One way to avoid the admission of incompetency is to argue that group meetings are simple matters and if other people would just be reasonable, mature adults, everything would work out easily.

The flight-taking from the complexity of group work becomes the basis for conventional wisdom, and many people develop a vivid yet unrealistic picture of an ideal meeting. This unrealistic "ideal meeting" causes many of us to expect a group to be able to do much more work than it possibly can in a given two-hour period. Since we expect too much, we often judge a meeting harshly and leave feeling that nothing was accomplished. A first step to productive work in a small group is to get rid of any unrealistic notions that we have of what a good productive meeting is like.

A business meeting, according to the unrealistic expectations, ought to be an efficient, no-nonsense matter. The planners should have a clear agenda; the members should adhere to the agenda and make all of their comments directly to the point under discussion in brief pithy statements that are expressed in clear language. All members should comment for about an equal amount of time (nobody should talk too much; nobody should talk too little); their statements ought to be relevant and productive. All messages should aid the group in its careful, step-by-step, reasonable deliberations. The members ought to be involved, eager-to-participate people who listen carefully and never get confused or lost.

The orderly, efficient meeting described above is a fiction largely found in quick-and-easy handbooks on how to learn to communicate in a meeting in thirty quick minutes of speed reading.

Real work groups do not have briskly conducted meetings in which the members march through the agenda with little discussion and rapid votes of approval. When a group has such a meeting it is conducting a rubber-stamping conference. The members are simply endorsing decisions that they have previously hammered out in meetings which were noisier, less directed, filled with departures from the agenda, and with moments of confusion. In the actual decision-making meetings some people talked more than others, and members often made rambling, beside-the-point comments.

We are not saying that some meetings are not better than others, but what we are saying is that you ought to judge a meeting in terms of a realistic picture of *how good work groups in fact operate,* not against some impossible ideal.

A Realistic Picture of Group Work

Group work takes time. Planners of a meeting often draw up an agenda for a group with enough work to keep one person busy all day and then expect five people working together to handle it in an hour or two. Temptations to overload an agenda are great. After all, getting busy people together for a meeting is often a major scheduling problem; why not take advantage of the fact that you have them all together to solve everything that you can think of at one time? The result of the long agenda is that the group fails to cover it properly. The members get bogged down on the first part or they race through the agenda without dealing with any topic adequately. The participants judging the group against the work goal set up by the overlong agenda come away feeling that the meeting was a failure.

What can you realistically expect of a good meetng? You must not expect five people to work as efficiently as one individual working alone. You ought not to expect the group to cover more topics in two hours than one person could study, consider, and decide on in thirty or forty minutes. You must allow sufficient time for the group to do the job! Remember, however, that participants will tend to take all of the time they can because of the group's tendency to put off difficult decisions until the last minute. Therefore, allow enough time, but set firm deadlines that force the group to come to decisions.

Those who wish to deny the complexity of small group communication often say at this point, "Well, if one person could do the job alone in so much less time, why have a meeting at all?" The answer is that if, indeed, the job is such that one person can do it alone *then you ought not to have a meeting.* We are measuring the amount· of work a group can realistically be expected to do in terms of individual work per hour, but we are applying that measure to work that requires a group effort. Remember, the meeting is an opportunity for specialists to come together to bring their knowledge to bear on an important matter. Unnecessary meetings *are* time wasters. People ought not to use meetings unless they are absolutely necessary. But when they are necessary, a good productive meeting is vital. Therefore, do not expect even a highly cohesive group with stable role structures and good work norms to solve more than one important problem or make more than one or two important decisions about which there are some serious differences of opinion in a single session.

Groups have short attention spans. Individuals tend to have attention spans measured in minutes, sometimes seconds. When you read, listen, or think about something, your mind often wanders. Groups, like individuals, have short attention spans. Extensive research in small group communication at Minnesota involved measuring (with a stopwatch) the length of time groups spent discussing a topic before they changed the subject. The remarkable feature about these data is their similarity. Whether the groups were composed of women in a Lebanese college, Japanese graduate students, university undergraduates, first-line managers at IBM, or educators in public health nursing, the average attention span for all groups was about one minute.

During any given period of the meeting, of course, individual listeners may or may not be attending to what is being said. Thus, the task of focusing everybody's attention on an idea is probably even more difficult than the evidence from studying group attention spans suggests.

Some failure to attend is probably a matter of individual listening habits, as we noted in Part I. Other failures to attend relate to group communication patterns. Generally, the group members will listen to a high status person more carefully than to a low status member. They will attend more to a member who has high esteem than to one with low esteem. When several people are fighting to control the channels of communication, or two are trying to assume the role of message source simultaneously, they often fail to attend to what the other is saying. People frequently wish to make a good impression. When they give up the floor they do not listen to the next speaker but, rather, try to think up something to say when they next get a chance to impress the others.

The emergent model of group work. Our expectation of a good meeting must be realistic. Our first step, therefore, is to replace any unrealistic picture of how groups work with a description of how they, in fact, do work. The basic principle is: *Decisions emerge from group interactions in the same way that roles emerge and normative behavior develops.*

The basic model of decision emergence in the small task-oriented group follows the process of the scientific emergent model we presented in Part I. Groups do not pick the best solution from an array of possibilities but rather tend to eliminate the worst, the not so good, and the fair, until they are left with several possible candidates, which they then struggle with until, finally, a decision emerges.

The process begins when someone submits an idea. Others contribute statements of fact, advice, and opinion. A number of ideas are displayed. Some information is rejected quickly and easily, just as some leader contenders are eliminated in the first phase of leadership emergence. The members accept some ideas just as quickly because of their source (i.e., the credibility of the member who submits them) or because all find the suggestion a good one. As the discussion continues, members sharpen their questions and discover areas of agreement. The group does not follow a rational step-by-step model of problem-solving at this point, becuase the members must find the areas of consensus and difference, the touchy points and the safe areas.

The members tend to approach the problem in its entirety at a rather superficial level, then return to the problem to dig in more deeply, swing away again, and return again to probe further.

After the first phase of easy elimination of ideas, the proponents of the solutions still in contention may put forward their answers once again. Others may now enter into agreement or disagreement with the contending solutions and tensions grow. Someone may introduce an aside which is completely off the topic or dramatize a fantasy theme. After some time has been spent chaining into the fantasy and releasing tension, someone may ask where the group is and what they are doing at this point. Other members may respond by suggesting the goals of the group, which enables the proponents of the contending solutions to mention them again. The group swings from problem to solution to goals to problem to goals to solution with tension release and group solidarity comments inserted throughout their deliberations.

At some point during this process, the group will discover that a decision has emerged, a decision to which they are committed and which they are willing to implement. Often the decision emerges without a vote or a formal show of consensus. (Sometimes the group may take a formal vote well after the decision has emerged.)

Realistic ways to organize group work. Quite often, groups like a relatively free and unstructured period early in the meeting to allow for a quick survey of the entire question and a chance to get some preliminary idea of the lay of the land. The group will often need some prodding to get down to confronting the important disagreements because of the typical flight-taking from tension. The leader or chairperson ought, therefore, to keep pushing the group to face up to tough questions. The pushing to task decisions, however, must be carefully timed, and the leader or chairperson should be alert to the needs for tension release. Once a decision emerges the group needs formally to state, confirm, and plan details to implement the decision. At the point when the decision has emerged, the group is ready for structure and an agenda. They will often march through the agenda items with little digression during the last stages of the problem-solving process even though they were highly resistant to such use of an agenda in the early phases.

Focusing a group's attention upon an idea so all members can understand it is a difficult task. Members have trouble keeping the thread of the discussion clearly before the group because of the group's short attention span. Yet group participants with an important decision to make will feel task pressure and want to get on with the job. They seldom tolerate the aimless free-associative pattern typical of conversation. If the group has an agenda, this forms a standard against which to judge orderly performance. Often the agenda becomes a liability because members keep commenting on the fact that the discussion is not sticking to the agenda, and then participants who have moved off the topic feel quilty. Members may also note that much of the agenda is still to be covered, and that puts pressure on the group to race along without satisfactorily working through issues.

All groups have something of a rhythm relating to the desire for relaxed and freewheeling discussion alternating with well-ordered and efficient marshaling of ideas and resources. The specific details of the rhythm tend to vary from group to group. A sense of timing in these matters is vital. You need to observe, experiment with, and be sensitive to verbal and nonverbal cues relating to the pulse of a given committee. Often the members of a group will provide nonverbal indicators that they are restless because of the restriction of the agenda. A participant might accept the suggestion that his comment is out of order in a grumpy fashion, sitting back in his chair with a frown. Another person may express confusion about the meaning of an agenda item or about what the group is supposed to be doing. Another may not want to proceed in the standard order. "I don't want to put this in the form of a motion or anything. Would it be all right if I just said something?" Verbal and nonverbal messages that express frustration with the procedure are important cues to tell the leader to deemphasize structure and forget the agenda for the time being.

Other verbal and nonverbal cues will indicate that a group has reached a point where it wishes structure. A member may simply suggest, "Let's cut out the talk and get down to business. What do we still have to do?" Participants may begin to look at their watches, shift in their seats, or say, "Question. Let's vote or something." At such a point, the chairperson or someone else in the meeting may suggest that they proceed in a more orderly way and the group will gladly move through the agenda. Their attention span as a group will continue to be short, but they will welcome any attempt to bring them back to the business at hand. When they are in a mood to kick ideas around they will resent the call for order.

Groups in an Organizational Context

Some groups are short-lived, like the ones in a small group communication class. Other groups are part of larger, well-established organizations which have a formal structure and an organizational culture composed of a mythology like the culture of a small group but on a much larger scale.

Formal structure. Often the student of small group communication sees the formal structure of an organization as so important and controlling in relation to the way people work together and in terms of the dynamics of small group communication that he or she wonders whether our descriptive group process applies in such situations. One of the important questions for us to consider, therefore, is how much does the formal structure of an organization modify what we have said in this book about small group communication?

Organizations attach clear nonverbal as well as verbal evidences to the status of positions. With a little study, outsiders as well as members can easily tell the status of a given position. Verbal titles may differ from organization to organization (director, manager, supervisor, unit chief, department head, project director), but the effect of status assignment is much the same. Nonverbal cues may also be different from organization to organization, but if you are alert you can soon learn how they indicate status. How are the desks arranged? What sort of desks do people have? Metal? Wood? Do they differ as to size? Where are the desks located? Are some desks in a large "bullpen" with many other desks? Are some closer together than others? Are some desks in separate offices? Are some offices carpeted? Such nonverbal cues indicate to both organizational members and visitors how important a given formal position is within the organizational structure.

Since the formal part of an organization is composed of positions with titles arranged to indicate their importance in the total organizational effort, one can plot it graphically. Such a visual chart is often called a table of organization.

Figure 5 presents a table of organization. Positions A, B, C, D, . . . J are managerial. The unlabeled positions are supervised by E, F, G, H, I, and J for specialists of various sorts whose efforts must be integrated into the total effort. Some of the specialists, for example those who work for supervisor B, are of a higher status in the organization than those supervised by people in positions F and G. (In fact, the specialists who work for manager B are of higher organizational status than managers F and G. They probably have a lot of special training and may be, for example, engineers, lawyers, or certified public accountants.)

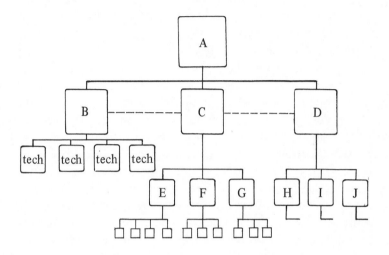

Figure 5 Table of Organization

People in organizations who are trying to work cooperatively together must solve two main problems. First, people must break up large-scale efforts into smaller tasks. Second, the specialized efforts of each small part must be fitted back together in an organized way. Organizing behavior solves the problem of dividing up work rapidly and efficiently despite employee turnover by using both a formal structure and an informal network of small task-oriented groups. We have seen in detail in Part II how small group communication results in role specialization. Here we examine how formal structure contributes to dividing up tasks.

Members of an organization usually spell out the kinds of work people who take each formal position are expected to do. If the job-related skills for a given position are widely used in other organizations, schools or training programs can prepare people for the work. For example, the skills required to play various positions on professional athletic teams are clearly spelled out and widely understood. If a baseball team needs a relief pitcher, it can trade for one with another team and be confident that the player can start his job immediately without on-the-job training. The same can be said of a football quarterback, a hockey goalie, or a basketball guard. In much the same way, people can be educated for formal positions as security guards or police officers, executive secretaries, automobile mechanics, registered nurses, computer programmers, and security analysts. If training in schools is not enough, older members of the organization can give on-the-job training to newcomers to develop the necessary skills for the job.

In the ideal situation, the formal organization would divide up the work in such a way that each position had the right amount of work so a capable person could do it working full time. If the position has less work than a good person can do, the result is a waste of personnel. If the position has more work than one person can do, that section of the organization falls behind and other divisions may have to wait to accomplish their tasks; the net effect is a loss of task efficiency.

A formal structure which evolves over a number of years tends to contain much wisdom accumulated by many trial-and-error efforts as well as from successful problem-solving attempts by individuals and groups. When an individual does not have full-time work, the organization may add duties to the position or combine several positions. When an individual has more work than can be accomplished, the supervisors may request new positions. Gradually, therefore, the specialization functions are incorporated into the formal structure. With the aid of the formal structure, the very complicated work of many organizations continues, with considerable efficiency despite frequent changes of personnel.

The second problem facing people trying to organize their efforts is that of putting the divided work back together into a total cooperative effort. A large number of individual tasks must be coordinated to build a bridge, create a product for a mass market, teach thousands of students at a college, take care of hundreds of patients at a hospital, or do any of the many large-scale projects of our contemporary organizations. The organizational structure solves the problem of coordinating effort by giving some formal positions the tasks of setting goals, dividing up work, setting deadlines for when the work will be brought together, and evaluating progress. Because the position of coordinator requires an overview of the various specialists doing part of the work, it is usually placed above the specialists in the structure. For our purposes we can think of the position of coordinator in a formal organization as being like the role of leader in the task-oriented small group. We will refer to these places in the organizational structure as positions of *formal leadership*. In Part III we discussed the relationship between formal leadership and natural emergent leadership in a small group. Our discussion of formal and informal leadership is most pertinent to the question of the relationship between formal structure and small group communication here.

The formal leadership positions serve as the places for praise and blame for successful or unsuccessful work within the organization. The organization tends to find job breakdowns and to try to correct them by going to the formal position and making the individual holding the position responsible. The organization will also reward the leadership position if a unit does unusually good work.

With responsibility, the person who fills a formal position of leadership usually gains the right to punish and reward the people within the unit. We refer to the right to punish and reward as *authority*. "Only the supervisor has the authority to fire him."

The formal leaders of an organization divide and integrate work within their units and coordinate their work with that of other units largely through communication. The formal organization, therefore, includes channels through which messages are to go to help people work cooperatively for common goals. The formal channels are important for the student of small group communication because they are the only way *official messages* can be transmitted. People cannot make official decisions over coffee in the cafeteria or in a bar after work. They may make the decision there for all practical purposes, but *they must then communicate that decision through formal channels to make it official.*

In Figure 5, the lines connecting the positions indicate the formal communication channels that characterize the organization. Position E is connected by a formal channel to position C. Position E is not connected by a formal channel to position A. Thus, communication aimed at position A from position E must first be transmitted to position C and then sent on to position A. A large number of investigations in laboratory situations where investigators set up networks restricting the flow of messages in a way that is like the restrictions imposed by formal channels in organizations, indicates that the shape of the network influences problem-solving and leadership emergence in small laboratory groups. People in positions B, C, D of Figure 5 have an advantage over people in positions such as E . . . J because they funnel messages from subordinates through to the individual in position A. The person in position C, for example, is in the center of a network which looks like Figure 6. Manager C, therefore, has an advantage in emerging as a leader of any task common to people in positions A, B, D, E, F, and G in terms of being the center of communication. Manager C is at a disadvantage, however, in that the person in position A is of higher organizational status and is the supervisor of position C. Positions B and D are of the same organizational status as C, and that is a complicating factor, but still the formal communication network favors the influence and leadership of any individual in position C.

Communication networks like the one outlined in Figure 6 are generally slow, inefficient, and frustrating if they are the only way people can communicate about task matters. (Remember our discussion now is only about the formal communication channels and the official messages. People, of course, do not stay in the straightjacket

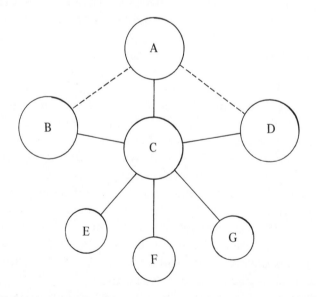

Figure 6 Formal Communication Network for Common Task-involving Positions A, B, C, D, E, F, G

of formal channels. We will discuss the informal channels later.) Other formal channels for official messages are needed for successful organizational problem-solving and decision-making.

Let us say that the leaders must make some important decision about a very large project that requires the resources of the total organization. They must bring the work of units lead by positions B, C, and D into coordination. The official meeting provides a way for individuals of varying status whose positions are not ordinarily connected by formal channels to communicate face-to-face. People in positions A, B, C, D, E, F, and G may meet in a small task-oriented group discussion and hammer out decisions in a setting which maximizes the possibility for good communication according to the model of the message communication style. In the meeting the members can provide feedback, achieve understanding, and, of considerable importance, come to assume informal roles in the group which may or may not reflect the formal structure of the organizational positions.

Because many organizations continue on through several generations of employees, they must deal with the continual turnover of participants. We have seen how the formal structure serves both to allow new recruits to learn their specialized job functions and to integrate the work into large-scale cooperative effort. Good organizations tend to modify the formal structure gradually and accumulate the wisdom of past experience and drop out those features which are no longer functional. New organizations can often learn from the experiences of old ones in similar situations and can pattern their formal structure on existing organizations when they begin.

The formal structures do, however, restrict the communication of members, and by further restricting the kinds of task functions a member can perform, they limit the way in which the dynamic model of role emergence and decision emergence can function in an organization. The status differences of formal positions often make it unlikely if not impossible for some members to talk with one another. People working in different units may be separated in other offices, even other buildings. Informal discussions among people of very high organizational status and people of very low organizational status are unlikely.

Nonetheless, even within the formal communication channels the business meeting serves as a way for people in positions of varying status and leadership and from different units to get together. Within such meetings the operation of the emergent model comes into play and informal roles may soon emerge which do not follow the organizational structure. If people in positions A, B, C, D, E, F, and G meet often, D may emerge as the leader of the group despite the fact that the person in position A is the formal leader of the unit.

Informal structure. If people were indeed interchangeable or standardized parts of mass-produced products like automobiles, they might be able to fit into the formal positions of our modern organization and not break out of the mold. However, individuals do differ in ways that affect their organizational behavior. The new manager does not do things in the same way as the old. The new manager assumes the authority, prestige, responsibility, and status that go with the position of formal leadership, but as we saw in Part III, the *way* the new manager exercises these role functions makes a good deal of difference. The formal structure is reinforced, discounted, and changed by the informal relationships which develop among people as they work together in the various groups that coalesce around natural leaders.

The informal groups may begin on a purely social basis and gradually start to take on task functions because the members have common organization-related objectives and they cannot communicate in a satisfactory way through the formal channels. Members may strike up informal channels purposefully to establish ways of communicating. Whatever the reasons for the formation of the informal groups, the dynamics of group formation discussed in Parts I, II, and III and the process of decision-making discussed in this section all apply to the operations of such groups. Thus, although the formal structure of an organization influences group process by restricting the flow of messages and, therefore, ruling out certain groupings, the formal business meetings and the informal groups that emerge do exhibit the same group dynamics.

In one sense, informal departures from the formal structure of an organization represent a blurring of the lines of control, of the communication channels, and of the dividing up of the work which has historically resulted from efforts to achieve common goals efficiently. Informal departures from formal structure make it more difficult for newcomers to "learn the ropes." When the organizational map fits the informal organizing behavior, then the new people will be able to work into the situation with less tension and wasted motion. Learning all the ins and outs, including skeletons in the closets, feuds, and personal relationships, requires time, effort, and tact. The newcomer must also be alert to the organizational mythology, to the fantasy themes which are still told at coffee, to the heroes and villains and good scenarios which are common to units and to the entire organization.

On the other hand, formal structures tend to be static. The demands placed upon the organization are ever changing and the static structure and formal channels of communication can seldom meet the changing needs successfully. The more rapid the changes an effective organization faces, the more flexible and important the informal channels of communication become.

Cooperative intergroup communication. The formal structure of an organization not only provides positions but often divides up the members into divisions or units. These organizational lines define insiders and outsiders, and members may well develop cohesiveness and loyalties to their units.

Since all of the units in the organization are supposedly working cooperatively together to do the organization's work, the communication context is ideal for high fidelity communication according to the model of the message communication style. If group representatives are in a cooperative situation, that fact should be made clear to all, and the possibility of feedback and improved listening can be enhanced. Even so, intergroup communication, even in cooperative situations, is more difficult for the most part than communication within a cohesive group. One important difference in the intragroup compared to the intergroup communication is the distance between source and receiver. Usually the channels of communication within a group are relatively available to all members in a face-to-face setting. Of course we have seen how the free flow of communication within a group is often restricted by status differences, cliques, and other work norms. When members of different organizational units try to work together, however, the available channels of communication are often restricted and the time delay between message and feedback may be increased. Communication often travels through intermediaries, and when a unit representative confers with a representative from another group, the member may distort the communication as he or she reports back to the group. Organizational status differences may intrude and make cooperative communication more difficult.

Competitive intergroup communication. Despite the fact that one might expect that units of the same organization would generally work cooperatively with one another, they often come into competition and conflict. Because the organizational structure sets up unit work responsibilities and assigns members to work in various sections, the boundaries of the units are clear-cut. The division has jurisdiction over certain duties, certain plant facilities, offices, machines, and so forth.

The internal dynamic of an organization encourages cohesive units to try to gain more members, more resources, and jurisdiction over more functions. The prestige of a given unit is often enhanced by its growth in size and control. The status and prestige of the formal leader also tend to grow with the size of the "empire." Since growth of one unit may be more rapid than growth of the entire organization, it must come at the expense of other units.

Recent discoveries about the conflict patterns among birds and animals serve to illustrate, if not explain, some of the intergroup conflict within organizations. According to the theory, birds and animals may be meek and cowardly at times and fight ferociously at others. The theory accounts for such behavior on the basis of an innate drive to defend territory. Each bird or animal stakes out an area, and when some other member of the species approaches its borders, the "owner" immediately attacks the intruder. The points of conflict, thus, tend to be at the borders of each group's "territory."

Members of organizational units do not have the same kind of "territorial rights" as the ranchers and homesteaders on television Westerns, but they do tend to treat the boundaries of their divisions as defining their turf. They often fight to protect their jurisdiction and territory. Thus, points of conflict tend to come at the border of each unit's symbolic territory.

One good way to view the organization is as a social system with its various units and divisions and informal groups in dynamic flux. Each individual, unit, and group responds to and affects every other individual, unit, and group in a complex, give-and-take fashion. The social system of an organization may reach a relatively balanced state in which the territorial boundaries of each group are stable and there is little chance for an "empire-building" group to gain much ground by aggressive action. When the system is in balance there is little intergroup conflict and competition. Modern organizations, however, tend to be unstable. Some of the change is planned. Just as units within the organization often exhibit a desire to grow, so do organizations within a larger social system. Profit-making organizations often strive to increase the size of their profit and try to gain a larger share of the market. Growth is a symbol of success, and growing groups gain in status and prestige. Most organizations have members who try to plan and change procedures to improve the work even when things are going quite well.

Much of the change affecting organizations is unplanned. Pressures from other organizations create challenges which need to be met. Calamity and catastrophe create crises. Organizations typically grow or contract. Organizations are open systems in the sense that there is a turnover of people because of promotions, retirements, resignations, and discharges. Adding new members and losing old ones adds uncertainty.

When an organization finds itself in a period of change the normal boundaries of units are also subject to change. If the organization extends its own boundaries, there is a larger turf for the units to occupy, and the more aggressive units rush in and come into conflict with one another. Stronger units may be tempted to take over some of the functions, resources, and personnel of weaker groups.

Just as units may come into competition and conflict as they scramble for the rewards of increased territory and jurisdiction, so they may collide as they try to escape blame. We have seen how the formal organization tends to assign blame for unsatisfactory task performance by making a formal position the center for praise or blame. In similar fashion, the organization tends to assign responsibility for task breakdowns to a unit.

When a number of units are working cooperatively on a large-scale task and something goes wrong they often indulge in highly defensive communication to ward off blame and guilt. The small task-oriented group meeting called to deal with a problem that cuts across organizational divisions may become a blame-assigning session in which each member defends his or her own unit while suggesting that the problem is really the fault of some other unit. Such meetings seldom do much to solve the organization's problems. Until the members agree on some common objective which they are willing to work for, and until they are willing to volunteer to help the larger good despite some sacrifices or some acceptance of blame by their units, such meetings will continue to be "time wasters" in terms of the ideal model of message communication.

We do not want to make light of the importance of the assignment of blame, the assumption of guilt, and the various ways the guilt can be purged within an organization. Blame and guilt are an important part of the organization's fantasies and play a big role in the mythology which serves to bind the members of the organization together and to give it an identity. We do not, as yet, know as much as we would like about the productive and unproductive ways that organizations handle blame and guilt. Professional baseball teams tend to assign the blame to a scapegoat, usually the manager, who they then sacrifice by a symbolic "firing." (They do not actually burn the sacrifice at the stake, but the term is suggestive.) Some consultants recommend that the members of an organization consciously try not to assign blame for failure and to focus instead upon the problem and how it can be solved. Whether human beings in an organizational context can, in fact, keep from assigning blame and assuming guilt is a question about which we have little evidence at the moment. Certainly we have ample evidence that people often do assign blame.

Generally, the result of competition and conflict among groups is to increase the within-group cohesiveness, and the social climate moves from the casual to the more grimly work-oriented. Each group becomes more highly structured and organized; the members demand more loyalty and conformity so they can present a united front against the enemy. The content of the internal messages includes fantasy themes which portray the insiders as heroes and the members of opposing groups as villains. Often one or two people from an opposing group will become the symbol of the entire group and the members will grow to have a personal dislike for those individuals.

The members celebrate the good parts of their unit and deny its weaknesses. They talk about the worst aspects of the competing groups and deny their strengths. The fantasy chains develop negative evaluations of the *others*: "They do not play fair like we do." "They play organizational politics, lie, cheat, do anything to get ahead." The emotional evocation of the fantasies tends to be hatred towards the others, and a general tone of anxiety, fear, rage, and hostility may characterize the dramas. The fantasy chains make it easier for members to keep their negative perceptions of the other groups and make it more difficult for them to correct their perceptual distortions.

When the results of competition are fed back into the organization, when one unit gets more new people, more office space, more resources than another, or when one unit gets jurisdiction over new functions at the expense of another, then the winners tend to become more cohesive, to enjoy the competition and conflict. Sometimes the winners begin to enjoy the new cohesiveness and social status so much that they become "fat and complacent" and neglect the task dimension. They become overconfident. The members are sure that they are best and that the other groups are not only bad but inept and so they can rest on their "laurels."

The losers chain into fantasies that often deny or distort the reality of their losing. They did not really lose. Some person in upper management made a bad decision, was misled, or pressured, or decided against them in some other unethical or unreasonable way. Blind luck or circumstances beyond anybody's control resulted in their failure.

If the group reevaluates its fantasies and accepts the loss, the members may splinter into hostile cliques; conflicts may come to the surface; blame may be assigned for the loss. The group may search for a scapegoat. The group becomes more tense and may be ready to work harder. The formal leader may have low cooperation from the members and may begin to drop concern for member needs and emphasize task matters. The spiral may continue with greater resentment, the formal leader may become a tougher taskmaster, and the fantasies may build a tradition of losing or a loser's culture for the group. If the group responds with scapegoating, cliques, and a tradition of losing, it becomes a punishing group for its members and it loses task efficiency as well.

Groups that lose in a competition with others need not become cripples. The members of the losing group can come to learn a good deal about the unit because the fantasies about the other groups and about their group as the best no longer account for the feedback that they are getting in response to their efforts and messages. The group may reexamine the situation and may enter a "lean and hungry" stage in which the members become more cohesive and dedicated and utilize their loss to improve their work and social norms.

Groups in Other Contexts

Negotiating groups. Our stress in this book has been upon the task-oriented small group which puts an emphasis upon cooperation among members to achieve a common goal and to share in the value achieved from their common success. We have noted the pressures which make for competition and conflict within groups which are ostensibly cooperative. Some groups, however, are clearly communication situations in which competition is emphasized. When representatives from two groups or organizations in conflict meet to work out an agreement despite the fact that they have conflicting goals, the result is a negotiating session.

The communication climate of a negotiating meeting puts a premium on misleading, confusing, and bluffing the other side. Neither the message nor the relationship style of communication is appropriate to the negotiating session. Where the relationship style emphasizes the honest expression nonverbally of internal feelings, the negotiating style emphasizes the nonverbal masking of internal feelings. The "poker face" and the "simulated tantrum" are useful nonverbal techniques when negotiators are testing one another with offers and counteroffers.

The high fidelity communication of the message model is inappropriate to negotiations where participants want to discover as much as they can about such things as the least amount that the other side is willing to agree to and how strongly the other side wants an agreement. Negotiators try to read between the lines, interpret inadvertent nonverbal giveaways, and make other assessments of the real "last offer" of the other side, and at the same time keep the opponents in the dark about their own objectives.

Our purpose here is not to provide you with a theory of negotiating communication but simply to note that groups sometimes meet around a table in a session which might on the surface seem to be a task-oriented cooperative group when, in fact, the people are bargaining and negotiating. Sometimes the meeting is ostensibly called for cooperative problem solving and it, in fact, becomes a negotiating session. As a student of small group communication you need to be able to discover the purposes of the session in order to use the appropriate style of communication.

Creative groups. Groups are sometimes used to dream up ideas and solutions. One of our colleagues was once invited to a session sponsored by a company producing food products. Along with a number of others from within and without the company he was served a meal of various foods synthesized from soybeans. After the meal the group was asked to think up an appropriate name for the product in order to make it palatable to the general public.

Alex T. Osborn developed one popular method of using groups for creative purposes, which he called *brainstorming.* He was at one time a member of the advertising firm of Batten, Barton, Durstine & Osborn and much interested in developing new ideas for advertising programs.

The rules for a brainstorming session are simple. The organizers get together a group of people, preferably with different back-grounds and interests, and give the group a problem or a creative task.

Briefly stated, the rules for a brainstorming session are as follows: (1) criticism is ruled out; (2) freewheeling of ideas is welcomed; (3) quantity of ideas rather than quality is emphasized; and (4) hitchhiking (adding onto) or modification of an idea is encouraged.

An interesting variation of the brainstorming session is the nominal group technique which grew out of research into the relative effectiveness of having a group of people brainstorm on the one hand and having the same individuals work alone on the same problem and pool their individual lists on the other hand. The research tended to indicate that individuals produced longer lists of ideas when working alone than they did in a brainstorming group. The nominal group works as follows: planners give the participants a period of time to think up ideas and write them down while sitting in the group. After a period of silently listing ideas the members begin to communicate and form an interacting group. They select a recorder and each person reads his or her list. The recorder puts the ideas down on a blackboard and flip chart, culling out the duplications until all the ideas are before the group. The members then begin to evaluate the ideas critically and pare down the list until a satisfactory solution emerges.

Public discussion groups. Public discussions are programs planned for presentation to an audience and are a special form of the ad hoc meeting discussed in Part I. Public discussions are held for a variety of reasons and take many forms. A discussion program may deal with education, social welfare, civil rights, urban problems, consumerism, politics, war and peace, or any number of public issues. Educators and broadcasters, among the most frequent users of public discussion, often use fresh approaches to the organization of programs and meetings. From buzz sessions to panel forms, from symposia to case studies, organizers of public discussions constantly search for a "gimmick" or some novel twist to create audience interest in their programs.

Generally, the discussion program differs from other forms of public speaking in its informality and in the number of participants. Informality tends to break down social tensions and allows the listeners to enjoy the interplay of ideas and personalities. Hand in hand with the informality of the discussion program goes a good deal of spontaneity. In our complex society the expert is a source of much information and advice, and the informal discussion program, particularly on television, gives the audience a chance to size up the individual expert.

Although the discussion program is often informal and strives for spontaneity, it is usually brief and well planned and organized. Good discussion programs balance careful planning with some freedom to depart from the agenda in order to assure spontaneity and to give the participants a chance to adapt to changing circumstances.

Public discussion programs may allow for audience questions and comments, in which case they are called *forum* discussions. Public discussions have a chairperson or moderator who introduces both the topic and the participants to the audience. The techniques for directing a meeting described in Part III are applicable to the moderating of a public discussion.

The opening part of the discussion program may be organized as a *symposium* discussion. In a symposium discussion the members divide the topic among themselves, and each member makes a brief comment about his or her subdivision of the topic after the moderator introduces the program. The opening speeches are usually carefully prepared, timed, and uninterrupted. Following the round of opening comments, the discussion may become a forum with everyone participating, or the discussants may take a few minutes to question one another about the content of their speeches.

The opening part of the discussion program may be organized as a *panel* discussion. In the panel discussion the participants all take part in discussing each point on the program outline. The atmosphere of the panel is less formal than that of the symposium, and the members interrupt one another as they aim to create the illusion of spontaneity and the give-and-take of a typical work meeting. The main difference between the panel discussion and a work group meeting is that the program is carefully planned as to agenda and the amount of time to be devoted to each portion of the outline. A good procedure is to devote about one-half of the program time to the panel discussion and then follow with a forum period.

A radio or television discussion is often in the form of a panel, sometimes with a studio audience and sometimes without. The participants often sit around the radio microphone or in a television studio, which allows them to speak informally with one another. Discussions are excellent ways to deal with important questions on radio and television. The informality and spontaneity of the format make for good listener interest. Over the years, particularly on television, informal discussion formats have grown in popularity when compared to prepared, formal public speeches.

$$*$$

A Brief Review of Key Ideas in Part IV

* The conventional wisdom often contains an unrealistic picture of good group work.

* A first step to productive work in a small group is to get rid of unrealistic notions about group efficiency.

* Groups, like individuals, have short attention spans.

* Real work groups do not have briskly conducted work meetings in which members march through an agenda.

* Temptations to overload an agenda are great.

* Overlong agendas result in the impression of group failure.

* Allow enough time for group work, but set firm deadlines to force the group to come to decisions.

* Unnecessary meetings are time wasters; use meetings only when absolutely necessary.

* Decisions emerge from group interactions as do roles.

* Important decisions emerge by the process of residues.

* Often decisions emerge without a vote or a formal show of consensus.

* All groups have a rhythm alternating relaxed and freewheeling discussion with well-ordered procedure.

* Organizations attach clear nonverbal and verbal cues to the status of formal positions.

* A formal structure which evolves over the years contains much accumulated wisdom from past experience.

* The formal structure allows the complicated work of an organization to continue with efficiency despite changes of personnel.

* *Formal leadership* refers to the organizational positions set up to coordinate effort.

* Formal communication channels carry official messages.

* The formal organizational structure is reinforced, discounted, and changed by the informal relationships among members.

* The dynamics of small group communication apply to the development of informal groups within the organization.

* Intergroup competition even in cooperative situations is common in organizations.

* Competition results from the drive for "empire" within an organization.

* Conflicts result when groups defend their turf from aggressive empire-builders.

* Conflicts result when groups try to escape blame for failures.

* Generally, the result of intergroup competition is an increase of within-group cohesiveness.

* Winning groups may become overconfident and fail in future competition.

* Losing groups often fantasize that they did not really lose.

* When losing groups come to accept their losses they often seek scapegoats for their failure.

* Losing groups may become more realistic in their analysis of the situation and grow more cohesive and effective.

* The communication climate of a negotiation puts a premium on misleading, confusing, and bluffing.

* Brainstorming is a technique for the use of groups for creative purposes.

* The most important features of brainstorming relate to the fact that criticism is ruled out and emphasis is upon quantity of suggestion rather than quality.

* Another technique for encouraging creativity is the nominal group, where members sit silently and think up ideas individually.

* Public discussions are programs planned for presentation to an audience.

* The discussion program differs from other forms of public speaking in its informality and in the number of participants.

* Forum discussions allow for audience participation.

* Symposium discussions begin with each member giving a brief opening comment.

* The panel discussion uses the give-and-take of a typical work meeting as the basic communication format.

Check Your Grasp of the Task Dimension of Groups

*(Complete all answers, then check
each answer on the pages given.)*

1. Describe the typical unrealistic picture of an efficient group meeting.

—pages 130 and 131

2. Describe the way groups actually go about doing good work.

—pages 131 to 134

3. Define a formal leadership position and contrast it with emergent leadership in a leaderless group discussion.

—pages 138 and 139

4. Describe the uses of formal communication channels in an organization.

—pages 139 to 141

5. Discuss the informal organizational structure.

—pages 142 and 143

6. List the forces within organizations which encourage intergroup competition.

—pages 144 to 146

7. Describe the general effects of competition on groups and the specific effects on winners and losers.

—pages 146 to 148

8. Describe the ways groups can be used to encourage creativity.

—page 149

CHECKLIST 1 – Before the Meeting

Put this checklist in a handy place and use it to plan every meeting:

1. What is the purpose of the meeting? Ritual? Briefing? Instruction? Consultation? Decision-making?

2. What are the outcomes to emerge from the meeting?

3. What type of conference will best achieve the purpose? Lecture and discussion? Short presentation by several people to be followed by discussion? Open discussion? Parliamentary meeting?

4. Who will participate? Have we left out someone who should be invited? Included someone who need not be involved?

5. Who will serve as leader?

6. Where is the best place to hold the meeting? What is a good time? How long should the meeting last?

7. How and when will the participants be briefed on the meeting and given directions for preparation?

8. What physical details need to be taken care of? Will the room be ready and open? Ventilation or heating? Audiovisual aids? Can we guard against unnecessary distractions? Refreshments advisable?

9. How will the proceedings and results be recorded?

10. Who will prepare the agenda? Will it be circulated in advance?

11. How will the meeting be evaluated?

12. What will be done to "follow up" and apply the results of the meeting?

(Additional "checks" of your own?)

CHECKLIST 2 – After the Meeting

Summary checklist for evaluating a meeting. May be used by an individual in the group or by an observer who reports to the group:

1. Was the preparation for the meeting adequate? Equipment available when needed and in working order? Necessary information furnished to members? Rooms? Visual aids? Physical requirements met?

2. Was the purpose of the meeting clear to all? Were objectives of the meeting clearly specified? Did the leader introduce the agenda clearly and concisely?

3. Was a permissive social climate established? Primary tension released? Did all members participate?

4. Was the nonverbal communication in tune with the purposes of the meeting?

5. Did the meeting stay on the agenda? Did the group have enough freedom really to work? Did the leader exercise the right amount of control? Did the participants keep their contributions short and to the point?

6. Did the meeting come to sound conclusions? Did the leader help the group reach a consensus?

7. How well did the leader handle difficult situations? The talkative person? The quiet member? Conflicts?

8. Were plans made to follow up and tie together the loose ends? In another meeting? In private conferences? By memorandums?

9. What three things can be done to improve the next meeting?

CHECKLIST 3 – Your Own Leadership

If you were the leader for the meeting, here is a checklist to see how well you "led" the meeting. Be honest with yourself; if you find a weak area, admit it and work to correct it for the next group meeting you must conduct:

1. Did you help dissipate primary tension? Were you friendly? Did you "loosen up" the group before plunging into the discussion?

2. Did you build group solidarity? Did your nonverbal as well as verbal communication indicate enthusiasm for the discussion and its importance?

3. Did you arrange the group so they could see and talk with one another? Did you invite latecomers to take a place that brought them into the discussion?

4. Did you make an opening statement, informally, suggesting that everyone is expected to take part?

5. Did you pose a challenging question to start the discussion? One that required thinking, not guessing, more than yes or no?

6. Were you patient? Did you give the group time enough to get acquainted? Did you listen to and respect the opinions and viewpoints of others, especially those who disagreed with you?

7. Did you let the group identify the issues and procedures and then guide them along the path they selected?

8. Did you construct "on-the-spot" thought-provoking questions?

9. Did you notice when the group had finished a topic, and then did you summarize for the group?

10. Did you refer questions back to the group instead of trying to answer them all yourself?

11. Did you talk less than 20 percent of the time?

12. Did you draw out the reticent person?

13. Did you tactfully handle the problem of the talkative and opinionated discussants? Did you balance participation among the discussants and tactfully discourage irrelevant discussions?

Sources

The best place to turn for additional information and a more complete and detailed analysis of small group communication along the lines laid down in this book is:

Bormann, Ernest G. *Discussion and Group Methods.* 2nd ed. New York: Harper & Row, 1975.

The sources referred to in the text are as follows:

Allport, Gordon W. *Pattern and Growth in Personality.* New York: Holt, Rinehart and Winston, Inc., 1961.

Bales, Robert F. *Interaction Process Analysis.* Cambridge: Addison-Wesley, 1950.

–––. *Personality and Interpersonal Behavior.* New York: Holt, Rinehart and Winston, Inc., 1970.

Cartwright, Dorwin, and Alvin Zander, eds. *Group Dynamics: Research and Theory.* 3rd ed. New York: Harper & Row, 1968.

Gibb, Jack R. "Defensive Communication." *Journal of Communication,* 11 (1961), pp. 141-48.

Hare, A. Paul. *Handbook of Small Group Research.* New York: The Free Press of Glencoe, 1962.

Howell, William S. "Motive Analysis for the Persuader." Chapter 15 in Bormann, Ernest G., William S. Howell, Ralph G. Nichols, and George L. Shapiro. *Interpersonal Communication in the Modern Organization.* Englewood Cliffs, N.J.: Prentice-Hall, Inc., 1969.

Lewin, Kurt. *Field Theory in Social Science.* New York: Harper & Row, 1951.

Lickert, Rensis. *New Patterns of Management.* New York: McGraw-Hill Book Company, 1961.

McGregor, Douglas. *The Human Side of Enterprise.* New York: McGraw-Hill Book Company, 1960.

Maier, Norman R. F. *Problem-Solving Discussion and Conferences: Leadership Methods and Skills.* New York: McGraw-Hill Book Company, 1963.

Maslow, Abraham H. *Motivation and Personality.* New York: Harper & Row, 1954.

Menninger, Karl. *Love Against Hate.* New York: Harcourt, Brace and World, Inc., 1942.

Shannon, Claude E., and Warren Weaver. *The Mathematical Theory of Communication.* Urbana: University of Illinois Press, 1949.

Shaw, Marvin E. *Group Dynamics: The Psychology of Small Group Behavior.* New York: McGraw-Hill Book Company, 1971.

Shramm, Wilbur L., ed. *The Process and Effects of Mass Communication.* Urbana: University of Illinois Press, 1954.

Stogdill, Ralph M. "Personal Factors Associated with Leadership: A Survey of the Literature." *Journal of Psychology,* 25 (1948), pp. 35-71.

———. *Handbook of Leadership: A Survey of Theory and Research.* New York: The Free Press, 1974.

Index

Ad hoc committee, 24-25
Agenda, 116
Allport, Gordon W., 59
Aping behavior, 56-57
Authority, 112

Bales, Robert F., 73
Berlo, David K., 8, 15
Brainstorming, 149
Briefing meeting, 24

Central persons, 106-107
Channels of communication, 15
    formal, 139-140
Cohesiveness, 48-49
    building of in groups, 58-67
    and conflict, 81-82, 88
    and pressures for conformity,
        57
Communication. *See also* Non-
        verbal communication
    channels of, 15, 139-140
    defensive, 29

through meetings, 23-27
    and intergroup competition,
        144, 146-147
    and systems theory, 144-145
Communication styles, 6-7. *See
    also* Conversion communi-
        cation style; Message com-
        munication style; Relation-
        ship communication style
    integration of, 14-15
    and small groups, 7-15
Communication theory, 6
    of conversion style, 13-14
    of message communication
        style, 9-10, 15-18
    of relationship style, 10-12
    small group, 15-21
Conflict management, 76-89
Conformity, 57
Confrontation in conflict, 79-80
Consciousness raising, 13, 14
Consultative meeting, 24
Conversion communication style,

7, 88-89
theroy of, 13-14
Creative groups, 149

Decision-making meeting, 24
Defensive communication, 29

Emergent model of group process,
    18-21, 52-56, 102-105,
    133-135
Empire building, 145-146
Esteem
    group rewards of, 65
    needs, 61
    in organizational context,
        112-113

Fantasy chains, 67-69, 146-147
Feedback
    and conflict, 83
    in message communication,
        9, 17-18, 21-22, 32-33
    nonverbal, 32
    in organizational meetings,
        141
    principle of explained, 9
    in relationship style, 10, 12
Flight-taking, 78-79, 83, 130
Formal channels of communica-
    tion, 139-140
Formal positions, 111-113, 136-
    139
Forum discussions, 150

Gay Liberation, 13
Geier, John, 55
Gender
    and conflict, 81
    and role emergence, 52-53

Group dynamics, 13
Group work
    emergent model of, 133-135
    realistic picture of, 131-132
    unrealistic picture of, 130-131
Groups
    agreements in, 74-75
    attention span of, 132-133
    cohesiveness of, 58-67
    and conformity, 57
    creative, 149
    disagreements in, 75-76
    evaluation of, 47-48
    fantasy chains in, 67-69
    negotiating, 148-149
    nominal, 149
    norms in, 56
    in organizational context,
        136-148
    primary tensions in, 73-74
    proper size for, 44-45
    public discussion, 150-151
    reminiscences of, 69-70
    research on, 49-50
    rewards of, 62-67
    rites and rituals of, 70
    role specialization in, 50-51
    secondary tensions in, 74
    social dimension of, 45-46, 72-83
    status in, 51
    T-groups, 12, 44
    task dimension of, 47, 82-89
    task-oriented, 44
    tensions in, 73-74
    test-tube, 50
    zero-history, 16-17, 18-19,
        24-26, 50, 81-82

Howell, William S., 59

Instructional meeting, 24
Intergroup communication, 144, 146-147
Interpersonal communication, 10

Leadership
  aids in emerging, 109-111
  ambivalence toward, 100
  and conflict, 77-79, 81
  contextual approach to, 101-102
  descriptive model of emergence, 102-109
  effect of appointing leader on, 108-109
  effect of changing members on, 108
  formal positions of, 111-113, 139
  natural versus formal, 113-115
  in one-time meeting, 25
  styles of, 101
  trait approach to, 100-101
Lewin, Kurt, 13
Lieutenant, 103-104, 105
Listening, 27-33
  active, 12
  and "shakedown cruise," 22

McGregor, Douglas M., 63
Manipulator, 107-108, 109
Maslow, Abraham H., 59
Mathematical Theory of Communication, The, 8
Meetings
  abuses of, 23
  kinds of, 23-26
  in the message communication

style, 23-27
  planning of, 26-27
  techniques for leading, 115-117
  use of, 23
Message, 15
Message communication style, 7-10
  meetings in, 23-27
  problems of, 21-23
  receiver in, 16, 28-31
  source in, 15
  theory of, 9-10, 15-18
Minnesota Studies of Small Group Communication, 21, 50, 55
Model
  of ideal conversion communication, 13-14
  of ideal message communication, 8-10, 15-18
  of ideal relationship communication, 11-12
  of leadership emergence, 102-109
  nature of ideal, 6, 7, 18
  nature of scientific descriptive, 6, 7, 18
  scientific emergent, 18-21, 52-56, 102-105, 133-135
Motivation, 59-62

National Training Laboratories, 13
Negotiating groups, 148-149
Nominal groups, 149
Nonverbal communication, 11, 135
  and feedback, 32
  in organizations, 136
Norms, 56-58

One-time meeting, 24-26
  evaluation of, 27
  planning of, 26-27
Organizations
  assigning blame in, 145-146
  authority in, 139
  and division of labor, 138
  empire bulding in, 145-146
  esteem in, 112-113
  and groups, 136-148
  informal structure of, 142-143
  and integration of work, 138
  nonverbal communication in, 136
  and status, 136
  and systems theory, 144-145
  and territoriality, 144
Osborn, Alex T., 149

Panel discussion, 151
Physiological needs, 60
Primary tensions, 73-74, 117, 119
Process of Communication, The, 8
Processes and Effects of Communication, The, 8

Receiver (in message communicationstyle), 16, 28-31
Relationship communication style, 7
  and conflict confrontation, 79-80
  nonverbal communication in, 11
  theory of, 10-12

Rites and rituals, 70
Ritualistic meeting, 23-24
Roles
  central persons, 106-107
  and gender, 52-53
  leadership emergence, 102-105
  lieutenant, 103, 105
  manipulator, 107-108
  process of emergence, 52-56
  specialization in, 50-51

Scapegoating, 80, 103
Scientific emergent model. *See* Model, scientific emergent
Secondary tensions, 74
  and conflict, 77-78, 119
Security needs, 60, 63
Self-disclosure, 12
Self-image, 12
Sex. *See* Gender
"Shakedown cruise," 22, 56, 103, 108
Shannon, Claude E., 8, 15
Shramm, Wilbur, 8, 15
Social needs, 60-61, 63-64
Source (in message communication style), 15
Status, 51-52, 61
  in organizations, 136
Students for a Democratic Society, 13
Symposium discussion, 150-151
Systems theory, 144-145

T-groups, 12, 44
Tensions. *See* Groups; Primary tensions; Secondary tensions

Territoriality, 144
Test-tube group, 50

Weaver, Warren, 8, 15
Women's Liberation, 13

Work groups. *See* Groups

Zero-history groups, 16-17,
   18-19, 24-26, 50, 81-82

EFFECTIVE SMALL GROUP COMMUNICATION

by Ernest G. Bormann, University of Minnesota
and Nancy C. Bormann, Normandale Community College

There is no easy, painless way to learn the complex nature of group dynamics. On the other hand, it is possible to gain practical knowledge of the topic without in-depth study of all recent research. The second edition of *Effective Small Group Communication* contains the same core of information about the dynamic process of good groups and about leadership which made the first edition a popular and successful text for courses in speech communication, psychology, education, and business and for workshops in continuing education.

The enlarged second edition contains new material on small group communication theory, the task dimension of group work, conflict management, listening, groups in the organizational context, fantasy and norm development, and the influence of cooperation and competition on small group communication.

The new edition retains the concise, concrete style of the first edition. Each of the sections ("Small Group Communication," "The Dynamics of Good Groups," "Leadership," and "The Task Dimension of Group Process") begins with a clear statement of objectives and concludes with a review of the key ideas as well as review questions with page references. Also included are three checklists covering meeting preparation, after-meeting evaluation, and self-evaluation for the group leader.

Group process is complex, but it is not difficult to understand as presented in this compact book. *Effective Small Group Communication* is appropriate for introductory courses in small group communication, for first courses in speech and communication which include units on discussion and group methods, and for concentrated courses and workshops in small group communication for members of businesses and organizations. The book is an excellent theory-plus-methods handbook for any course employing the small-group approach to learning.

ABOUT THE AUTHORS

Ernest G. Bormann received his Ph.D. from the University of Iowa. He is currently professor of speech-communication at the University of Minnesota. Among Dr. Bormann's recent publications are *Discussion and Group Methods,* 2nd ed., Harper & Row, 1975, and (with William S. Howell) *Presentational Speaking for Business and the Professions,* Harper & Row, 1971. Nancy C. Bormann received her M.A. from the University of Iowa and is an instructor at Normandale Community College. The Bormanns are also co-authors of *Speech-Communication: A Comprehensive Approach,* 2nd ed., published by Harper & Row.

Burgess Publishing Company   Minneapolis, Minnesota 55415